DECODING

DIVINE

WEALTH

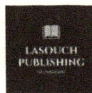

LASOUCH
PUBLISHING

LasouchPublishing.com

Decoding Divine Wealth

DECODING DIVINE WEALTH

*Unlocking Heaven's Blueprint
for Supernatural Abundance
and Kingdom Prosperity*

BISHOP RICHARD
ASAMOAH BOATENG

DECODING DIVINE WEALTH: Unlocking Heaven's Blueprint for Supernatural Abundance and Kingdom Prosperity

Published by:
LASOUCH PUBLISHING: 11355 Richmond Ave, Houston TX, 77082, US.
+1 (917) 594-7014, +2348058092923
www.lasouchpublishing.com

ISBN-13: 978-1-7638902-0-6

Unless otherwise indicated, Scripture quotations are from the King James Version (KJV), New King James Version (NKJV) and the New International Version (NIV) of the Holy Bible. Scripture quotations identified NIV are from, The New Scofield Study Bible, New International Version, Copyright © 1984 by Oxford University Press, Inc. Scripture quotations identified KJV are from the New Marked Reference Bible, the King James Version, Copyright © 1964, 1972 by ZONDERVAN PUBLISHING HOUSE.

TABLE OF CONTENTS

Table of Contents

Table of Contents

DEDICATION

To **Sabina Arthur**,

My beloved mother-in-law,

Your unwavering strength, godly wisdom, and relentless faith have been a pillar in our family and a testament to generations.

Thank you for modeling grace, perseverance, and quiet power—the kind that does not demand attention but commands respect.

You have taught us, not only with your words, but with your life—how to love deeply, give generously, serve faithfully, and trust God unshakably.

I honor you today for the seeds of faith and legacy you have sown.

May this book reflect a portion of the spiritual wealth you've imparted.

With deep love and gratitude,

Bishop Richard Asamoah Boateng

ACKNOWLEDGEMENTS

To my beloved wife, **Lady Rev. Evelyn Asamoah Boateng—**

You are my partner in life, ministry, and destiny. Your unwavering support, fierce loyalty, and deep spiritual insight have been a constant source of strength and inspiration throughout this journey. Thank you for standing beside me, praying with me, and believing in the vision long before it became visible. Your quiet sacrifices, wisdom-filled counsel, and unconditional love continue to empower and sharpen my assignment.

This book bears your fingerprints. You have been the wind beneath my wings and the steady force that anchors my calling. I honor you not only as my wife but as a Kingdom woman of valor.

13

To my amazing children, Alex. Godgiveson, Chelsea, Princess, Jasmine and Richie —

You are my pride and joy, my living legacy. Your love, patience, and understanding have allowed me to pursue the call of God with boldness and focus. Thank you for cheering me on, for the joy you bring, and for reminding me daily why legacy matters. You inspire me to keep building, to keep writing, and to keep pressing forward.

May you always walk in divine wisdom, multiply grace, and carry the mantle of Kingdom greatness far beyond what I have seen.

With all my heart,

Bishop Richard Asamoah Boateng

PREFACE

An Invitation to Prosper on Purpose

There comes a time in every believer's journey when mere survival is no longer enough—when the soul begins to cry out for **significance, stewardship,** and **supernatural alignment**. That time, for many, is now.

Decoding Divine Wealth was not written as just another book on Christian finances. It is a prophetic blueprint—a divine assignment to pull back the veil on a mystery that has kept generations of believers confined to cycles of insufficiency, even while sitting under open heavens. This is a clarion call to the body of Christ to arise—not just in prayer or in power—but in **financial dominion with eternal purpose**.

For years, wealth has been misunderstood in spiritual spaces. We've seen the idolization of riches in some corners and the glorification of poverty in others. Both extremes have left the Church disempowered and disengaged from major spheres of influence. But God is shifting the narrative. He is raising a remnant—**sons and daughters who will carry wealth like a weapon and a witness**. Not to boast, but to build. Not to hoard, but to heal. Not to flaunt, but to fund Kingdom advancement.

This book was conceived in prayer, forged through revelation, and written for reformers—people who feel the pull to fund revival, break the back of generational poverty, and live as vessels of God's divine abundance.

You'll find that this book doesn't just inform—it transforms. It doesn't flatter—it challenges. It doesn't conform to worldly formulas—it aligns with timeless Kingdom principles. The revelations contained here will shake your theology, upgrade your expectations, and reposition your thinking. But more than anything, they will **call you into covenant consciousness**—into a relationship with wealth that is sacred, strategic, and Spirit-led.

So as you begin, I invite you not just to read but to **engage**. Let the Spirit of God deal with mindsets that no longer serve your destiny. Let Him expose belief systems inherited from religion, culture, or fear. Let Him awaken dreams, stir boldness, and sharpen vision. As you turn each page, I pray that your eyes will be enlightened, your hands will be equipped, and your spirit will be reignited for the journey ahead.

Because this is not just a book.

It's a prophetic mirror, a Kingdom roadmap, and a financial altar.

Welcome to a life of divine wealth—decoded, demystified, and deployed for Kingdom impact.

This is your moment. Don't read it casually. Read it as if your generation depends on it. Because it does.

INTRODUCTION

Why Divine Wealth Must Be Understood, Not Just Prayed For

What would your life look like if you never again feared lack? What would happen if believers stopped reacting to money and started ruling with it?

What if you realized that **wealth isn't just for the elite—it's for the obedient?**

We are living in a time of divine transition. Across nations, God is raising voices, visions, and vessels to shape culture and reform broken systems. But while many are gifted, anointed, and passionate, they are also financially paralyzed. Dreams are delayed not because of a lack of calling, but because of a **lack of understanding about divine provision.**

Introduction

That's why this book exists.

Decoding Divine Wealth is not just a how-to guide for Christians trying to get rich. This is not a prosperity gospel pitch, nor is it a religious condemnation of abundance. It is a Spirit-led reintroduction of wealth—**not as a luxury, but as a language of purpose.** Not as a worldly trophy, but as a **tool of transformation.**

Throughout the chapters of this book, you'll learn to:

- **Understand money as a covenant expression**, not just a medium of exchange
- **Break demonic and cultural mindsets** that sabotage prosperity
- **Distinguish between riches and wealth,** and why the latter requires spiritual maturity
- **Heal your soul** so it can safely carry the weight of divine supply
- **Create biblical and practical structures** to sustain overflow and fund Kingdom vision
- **Live as a Kingdom financier**, with spiritual intelligence and generational relevance

We'll uncover how **your financial health is connected to your spiritual wholeness,** and how God desires you to carry resources **not for self-glorification, but for global transformation**.

This book is written for:

- The believer tired of religious clichés and ready for results
- The leader called to impact cities but struggling with scarcity
- The entrepreneur with vision but no visible backing
- The minister ready to move from fundraising to faith-fuelled resourcing
- The everyday child of God who dares to believe there's more

Each chapter is a conversation between your **calling and your capacity**. You will be challenged. You will be stretched. You will be reintroduced to yourself—not as someone seeking provision, but as one **entrusted with the power to produce it** through divine alignment and obedience.

You are not reading this by accident.

Introduction

This is a divine setup—a summons into your next financial dimension. A line is being drawn between the survival of yesterday and the supernatural supply of your tomorrow.

So read slowly. Pause to reflect. Pray while reading. Journal your shifts. Because the Holy Spirit will not only teach you through this book—He will activate you.

You're not just about to understand divine wealth. You're about to walk in it, live through it, and **multiply it for the glory of God**.

Let the decoding begin.

Bishop Richard Asamoah Boateng

Presiding Bishop; Destiny Impact Worship Centre

CHAPTER 1

UNDERSTANDING WEALTH

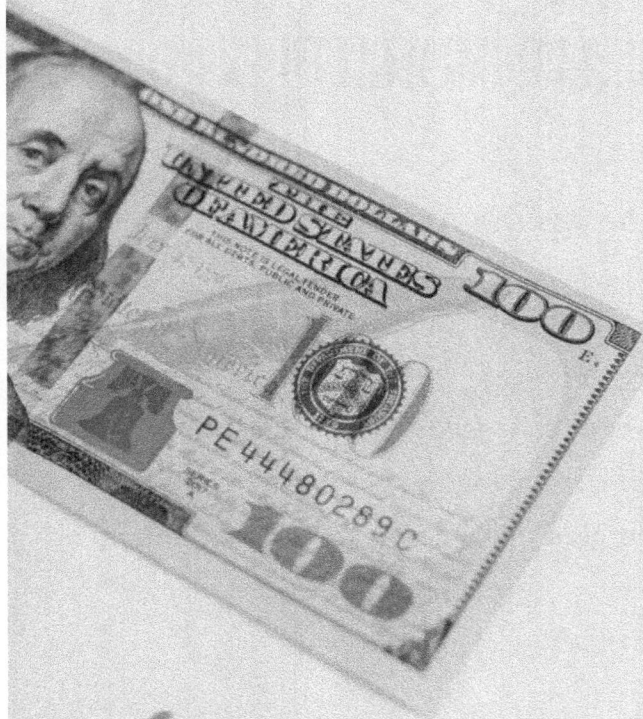

CHAPTER ONE

UNDERSTANDING WEALTH

Breaking the Myths Around Money

Many believers today harbor a skewed understanding of money—one that has subtly hindered their financial freedom and purpose. For some, wealth is automatically equated with worldliness, while for others, poverty is mistaken for piety. Phrases like, *"Money is the root of all evil,"* are misquoted and misinterpreted, fuelling a mindset that subtly resists prosperity.

But what does the Bible really say?

The actual verse in 1 Timothy 6:10 reads, *"For the love of money is the root of all evil..."*—not money itself. Money, in its purest form, is neutral. It is a tool, not a god. What corrupts is not the presence of money, but the posture of the heart toward it. When money becomes the object of obsession, compromise creeps in. But when money is seen as a servant, subject to God's will, it becomes a powerful force for impact.

God is not intimidated by your financial success. In fact, Scripture affirms that He *"takes pleasure in the prosperity of His servant"* (Psalm 35:27, NKJV). He is not glorified by your lack—He is glorified when you use what He's given you to fulfil your assignment on earth. Your prosperity, when channelled rightly, becomes a megaphone that declares God's faithfulness.

In our world today, we are familiar with the stigma that sometimes surrounds wealth—particularly within the Church. Yet, a biblical worldview teaches us that true prosperity is not about flaunting riches, but about advancing the Kingdom, lifting communities, and leaving a godly legacy. If your rising leads to lives being transformed and God's name being glorified, then your prosperity is not just permitted—it is necessary.

Contrary to popular portrayal, Jesus was not destitute. He had resource handlers—Judas Iscariot served as treasurer for His ministry (John 13:29). At His birth, kings from the East brought Him gold, frankincense, and myrrh—gifts of significant value. Even the soldiers who crucified Him gambled for His robe, described as *"seamless, woven in one piece from top to bottom"* (John 19:23), a garment fit for royalty.

Jesus paid taxes (Matthew 17:27), fed multitudes, and provided for His disciples. He operated from a realm of supernatural supply and financial stewardship. His life model shows us that being anointed doesn't mean being broke—it means being resourced for your assignment.

In the church today, it is vital to redefine what we see as "godliness." Jesus wasn't poor—He was purposeful. His wealth was functional, not flashy.

God's Pattern for Wealth in Scripture

From Genesis to Revelation, the Bible is filled with examples of God's people walking in exceptional wealth—without compromising their faith. Solomon wasn't just wealthy; he was *the richest king in history*, and it was God Himself who granted him such abundance (2 Chronicles 1:11–12). David, his father, left behind vast resources for the building of the temple. Abraham, the father of faith, had servants, livestock, and silver and gold in abundance (Genesis 13:2). Isaac prospered until he became *"very wealthy"* (Genesis 26:13), and Jacob left Laban's household with great possessions. Even Job, who endured severe testing, was restored with twice as much wealth as he had before.

These were not godless men—they were covenant carriers. They were flawed humans, yes, but men who walked with God. So, who told you that serving God disqualifies you from financial greatness?

If God could entrust wealth to those who honored Him in ancient times, how much more in this dispensation of grace, when we have access to both the Abrahamic blessing and the redemptive benefits of Christ?

One of the greatest mistakes believers make is underestimating the power of money. Money is not just paper or coins—it is a medium of exchange, a carrier of value, and a tool of influence. In spiritual terms, money is a resource that can either serve the kingdom of darkness or the Kingdom of God, depending on whose hands it is in.

In Africa, where economic challenges are real and widespread, we must rise above survival thinking. We must begin to **value money** as a divine enabler—not to worship it, but to steward it. Money answers to purpose. It builds churches, funds missions, feeds families, pays school fees, drives innovation, and empowers transformation.

The earlier we stop despising wealth and start seeing it as God sees it, the sooner we'll begin to unlock divine ideas, supernatural provision, and generational impact.

Have you noticed that Jesus spoke about money and possessions more than He did about heaven and hell combined? That's because He understood the spiritual and practical influence of money. Money isn't just a financial issue—it's a **heart issue**. Wherever your treasure is, there your heart will be also (Matthew 6:21).

Even the gospel, though freely given, requires financial backing to be distributed. Imagine trying to run a crusade, organize a radio broadcast, support your local church, or even transport Bibles into rural communities—without money. It's virtually impossible.

From transport to food, accommodation to media, church rent to outreach materials—money is a necessity in ministry. And God knows this. That's why He desires to empower His children financially—not just for personal comfort, but for Kingdom advancement.

Addressing Fear, Worldliness, and the Heart

There's a dangerous belief that still lingers in many religious circles—that wealth is the exclusive domain of unbelievers, and that spiritual people must remain poor to prove their devotion. Some even fear that gaining wealth will automatically lead to spiritual decline.

But let's be clear: it is not **money** that makes people fall—it is a heart that was never truly surrendered to God in the first place. Wealth doesn't change you; it reveals you. It exposes what was always hidden in your priorities, character, and desires.

This fear-driven theology has crippled many sincere Christians, especially in Africa, where scarcity has often been spiritualized. As a result, many believers shy away from financial ambition, thinking it's ungodly to aspire for wealth.

But God's Word challenges this lie. He wants His children to rise as financial stewards—men and women who know how to handle wealth with humility, integrity, and Kingdom vision.

Decoding Divine Wealth

Yes, God desires that you prosper—abundantly. But divine prosperity comes with divine purpose. Your wealth should never pull you away from God; it should pull others toward Him.

In Luke 12, Jesus spoke of the rich man who expanded his barns but had no thought of God or eternity. That man died suddenly and was called a *"fool"* because he was rich in possessions but bankrupt in purpose.

Your prosperity must serve heaven's agenda. It must fund missions, uplift the needy, support your local church, and enable divine assignments. When your riches become instruments of righteousness, God will trust you with more.

Our continent needs believers who can rise financially and remain spiritually grounded. We need Kingdom financiers—men and women whose wealth flows with worship, generosity, and eternal impact.

Deuteronomy 8:18 is a prophetic cornerstone for every believer called to prosper: *"But thou shalt remember the Lord thy God: for it is He that giveth thee power to get wealth..."*

God doesn't just give wealth—He gives the **power to get wealth**. That power manifests through divine ideas, business opportunities, spiritual favor, uncommon access, and wisdom for value creation.

In the African setting, where unemployment and economic hardship are rampant, this verse becomes a beacon of hope. It tells us that God is not just the God of heaven—He is the God of empowerment. He gives us the ability to rise through innovation, diligence, faith, and integrity.

So stop waiting for money to fall from the sky. Ask God to awaken the wealth-creating potential inside of you. You were not born to beg—you were born to build.

The Mindset and Mouth of the Wealthy

If you are going to walk in divine wealth, it all begins with your mind. As Romans 12:2 declares,

> *Be transformed by the renewing of your mind."*
> **Romans 12:2**

Until your mindset changes, your money will not.

Start seeing money the way God sees it:

> – Not as a master to be worshiped, but as a servant to be deployed.

– Not as a source of identity, but as a resource for assignment.

– Not as a status symbol, but as a Kingdom tool.

In many cultures, money is often idolized or feared. But God is calling His children to break free from both extremes—poverty theology and prosperity idolatry—and embrace a healthy, balanced Kingdom mindset.

Your wealth must never define you. You define your wealth. You command it, control it, and assign it. The moment money begins to master your emotions, your faith, or your identity, you've crossed a dangerous line.

One of the most powerful tools God has given you to access wealth is **your mouth**. Proverbs 18:21 reminds us that *"Death and life are in the power of the tongue."* If you keep declaring lack, you will keep experiencing it. If you confess shortage, you'll attract it.

It's time to change your confession.

Stop saying:

"I'm broke."

"Things are hard."

"I can't afford it."

Start declaring:

> "I am blessed and highly favored."
>
> "Money flows to me in abundance."
>
> "I am a wealth distributor in the Kingdom."
>
> "I have more than enough to fulfill my divine purpose."
>
> "I am empowered to create value and attract resources."
>
> "I am a solution to financial hardship in my generation."

In our world today, where economic pressure tempts many to speak negatively, this is a spiritual discipline. Your words shape your world. Don't just think wealth—**speak it** with authority. Declare God's promises until your environment aligns.

Wealth begins within. Before it shows up in your bank account, it must first manifest in your mindset, your posture, and your attitude. Begin to **walk like someone who carries destiny**. Plan like someone who expects results. Dress with dignity and excellence. Speak with conviction and vision.

Believe God for great things—not as wishful thinking, but as your covenant right.

Greatness is not arrogance. Confidence in God's promises is not pride. When you carry the wealth of divine revelation, walk with the excellence that matches it.

This is not about pretending—it's about aligning. Align your habits, your faith, your budget, your language, and your relationships with the level you're believing God for.

God wants you to prosper—not for vanity, but for vision. Wealth is a divine empowerment to fulfill your assignment, bless others, and expand God's Kingdom. But before you see money in your hands, you must first see it clearly in your spirit.

Renew your mind. Correct your theology. Align your words. Position yourself for divine increase.

Your wealth journey begins here.

CHAPTER 2

THE POWER TO GET WEALTH

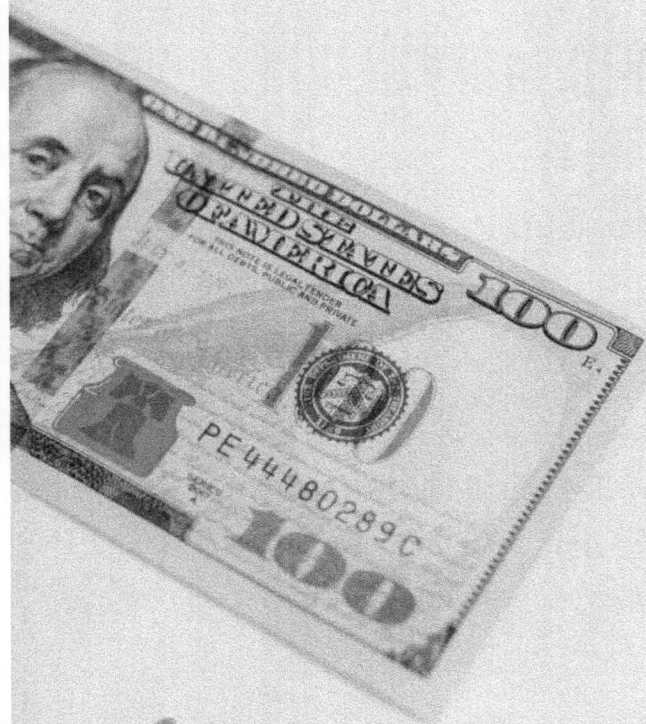

CHAPTER TWO

THE POWER TO GET WEALTH

Wealth Begins with Power, Not Paper

Across Africa—and indeed around the world—many believers passionately pray for financial breakthrough. They fast, sow seeds, and anoint themselves with oil, crying out for divine intervention in their finances. And while prayer and giving are powerful spiritual disciplines, they were never intended to **replace** responsibility, wisdom, and value creation.

God doesn't rain naira, cedis, dollars, or rand from heaven. He doesn't throw paper money from the skies. What He gives is **power**—power to get wealth (Deuteronomy 8:18).

That power manifests in ideas, favor, skills, diligence, and discernment. Wealth, in God's system, is the fruit of divine empowerment combined with intentional action.

Miracles open doors, but it is your preparation and application that sustains provision.

When God gives you the power to get wealth, it often shows up wearing the clothes of **responsibility**. It may look like a divine idea that needs nurturing. It may arrive as a business opportunity, a problem you're called to solve, a natural talent, or a new relationship.

Unfortunately, many are praying for money while walking past their answer every day.

You must develop **spiritual discernment** to recognize God's wealth-delivery systems in your life. That power might be in your ability to write, teach, organize, bake, farm, consult, design, counsel, or lead. You don't need more money—you need to **discover and activate your power base**.

The question is not, "Where is my money?" The question is, "Where is my power to get it?"

Decoding Divine Wealth

There's a vast difference between **miracle money** and **covenant wealth**—and every serious believer must learn to distinguish the two.

Miracle money is God's short-term intervention to meet a pressing need—perhaps you're stranded, facing eviction, or urgently need school fees for your child. In such moments, God may send unexpected help, just like He fed Elijah through ravens (1 Kings 17). But that's not His long-term plan for your finances.

Covenant wealth is different. It is sustainable. It is generational. It is built on principles, discipline, stewardship, and obedience. God wants you to move from living on miracles to operating by covenant. From depending on daily manna to owning the land that produces harvests.

Miracles are survival mechanisms. Covenant is a wealth system.

The covenant of wealth doesn't operate through wishful thinking—it operates through **obedience**. To walk in covenant wealth, you must:

- Obey divine instructions
- Work diligently in your area of calling

- Practice consistent generosity
- Maintain financial discipline
- Develop a long-term mindset

These principles are not just spiritual—they are practical. Covenant wealth demands a lifestyle, not a lucky moment. It asks you to **honor God with your substance**, steward your increase wisely, and grow in financial intelligence.

In our society today, where quick fixes are often idolized, this truth is crucial: **Sustainability is built, not stumbled upon.** The question is not if God wants to bless you—the real question is whether you're ready to **build what He blesses**.

The Covenant Path—From Process to Possession

When God placed Adam in the Garden of Eden, He didn't hand him a ready-made mansion or a collection of luxury items. He gave him a **garden**—a raw environment filled with untapped potential. The trees needed pruning. The soil needed tending. The animals needed naming. God provided **resources**, but He expected **responsibility**.

Likewise, many believers today are praying for chairs when God has already given them wood, tools, and creative intelligence. The power to get wealth is hidden in your **ability to recognize raw materials** and turn them into value.

What skill, idea, or connection has God placed in your "garden"? Are you managing it or ignoring it?

In Africa, many live surrounded by opportunity yet miss it because they're waiting for something polished instead of stewarding the raw. **God's provision often comes wrapped in responsibility.** What you do with the raw determines what you reap in reward.

Joseph's rise to influence and wealth was not instant—it was the result of **faithfulness through process**.

He served with excellence in Potiphar's house, despite being a slave. He interpreted dreams in prison, though he was forgotten. When Pharaoh summoned him, Joseph didn't just interpret a dream—he presented a **national economic strategy** that saved Egypt from famine.

God didn't drop money into Joseph's lap. He gave him **wisdom, favor, and positioning**—and Joseph **used those gifts** to create national impact and personal elevation.

This is a Kingdom pattern: God promotes people who prepare in private and solve problems in public.

You may be in your "Potiphar phase" or your "prison season" right now, but remain excellent. Be diligent. Develop your gifts. Because when opportunity calls, it is those who are prepared that rise.

David's journey to kingship was paved with process, pressure, and preparation.

Before the crown ever touched his head, he had already killed lions and bears in obscurity. He stood boldly before Goliath when others trembled. He served a jealous Saul with honor. He led rough men in caves, turning fugitives into fighters. He worshipped in the wilderness and sought God for strategy at every turn.

God was not delaying David—He was **developing** him.

In the same way, your wealth journey may be filled with tests, trials, and seasons of waiting. But don't despise the process—it's in these moments that God sharpens your leadership, deepens your trust, and expands your capacity.

Covenant wealth is not just about money—it's about maturity. God is more interested in the kind of person you're becoming than the kind of things you're acquiring.

Deuteronomy 8:18 tells us the purpose behind divine wealth: *"…that He may establish His covenant which He swore to your fathers…"*

God empowers you financially **so that** His covenant purposes can be fulfilled on the earth. Wealth is not given just for your comfort—it is given for **Kingdom advancement**.

If your vision doesn't include the poor, the gospel, the Church, and the next generation, then it's too small.

Your business is not just a hustle—it's a channel. Your promotion is not just a reward—it's a platform. Your increase is not just a blessing—it's an assignment.

In Africa and beyond, God is raising Kingdom financiers—men and women who will feed nations, fund revivals, build schools, support churches, and disciple economies. Are you willing to be one?

Activation Through Obedience and Stewardship

When God releases the power to get wealth into your life, it is your responsibility to steward it wisely. Power that is ignored becomes potential that is never realized. Grace that is mismanaged leads to frustration.

It's possible to be deeply anointed, yet financially stagnant. Gifted in prophecy, worship, or leadership—yet unable to sustain basic needs. Called by God, yet hungry and dependent. Why? Not because God failed—but because the individual failed to **manage what God entrusted**.

Across the world, many pastors, musicians, teachers, and intercessors are drowning in poverty—not due to a lack of calling, but due to a lack of systems. They have passion, but no plan. Fire, but no structure.

Anointing must be married to administration. Talent must be partnered with strategy. Grace must be governed by stewardship.

God will never bypass your role in the manifestation of your own wealth. He gives you power—but you must **put that power to work**.

Decoding Divine Wealth

The power to get wealth is like a dormant seed. It carries immense potential, but that potential must be **activated** through obedience, diligence, and faith.

You activate this power by:

- **Believing** what God has said about you and your prosperity
- **Acting** on divine ideas without procrastination
- **Planning** with wisdom and seeking godly counsel
- **Executing** your vision with excellence
- **Remaining consistent**, even when results are slow to show

Activation requires motion. God multiplies what you move toward. Your faith must have corresponding action, or it remains ineffective (James 2:17).

Many believers in our generation suffer from "revelation paralysis"—they receive prophetic insight, attend powerful conferences, get downloads during prayer, but fail to take the **next courageous step**.

Don't die with activated power still sitting inside you. Rise up. Move forward. Do something with what God has already given you.

The Power to get Wealth

The journey into covenant wealth doesn't begin with millions—it begins with **faithfulness in the mundane**.

Can you manage N10,000 with integrity before God can entrust you with N10 million? Can you be trusted to show up on time, to build with excellence, to handle tithes, to bless others, even when your income is small?

The parable of the talents in Matthew 25 teaches us that **increase comes to those who multiply what they already have**. God blesses stewardship. He rewards responsibility. He opens doors for those who protect and invest what they've been given.

Opportunities don't always come with announcements. Sometimes they arrive as problems to solve or small tasks to complete. When you treat the little things like big things, you qualify for the bigger things.

In our African context, where many are waiting for a "breakthrough," the real breakthrough often lies in being faithful, resourceful, and fruitful right where you are.

Value Creation—The True Currency of Wealth

In both spiritual and economic realms, **money follows value**. If you are not solving a problem or meeting a need, your prayers for financial increase may remain unanswered—not because God is unfaithful, but because wealth requires a **value exchange**.

The wealthy are not necessarily the most prayerful, but they are the most **impactful** in their space. They offer something tangible, helpful, or transformational—whether it's a product, service, skill, or idea.

If you want to attract wealth:

- Become a solution to someone's problem
- Learn to serve people with excellence
- Position your gift to meet a real need
- Develop competence and consistency

In the church today, we have brilliant minds, yet many die in lack because they were never taught how to **package their value**. Some are gifted tailors, teachers, caterers, musicians, writers, or farmers—but they haven't linked their skill to systems or service.

The Power to get Wealth

Wealth is waiting for you at the intersection of your **gifting and service**.

Even Jesus, the Son of God, built His ministry through **service**. He healed the sick, cast out devils, fed the hungry, taught the multitudes, raised the dead, and restored broken hearts. He didn't manipulate people—He met their needs.

This is why the crowds followed Him—not just because He was anointed, but because He was **relevant**.

If Jesus served, how much more should we?

There is no Kingdom wealth without Kingdom service. Your rise must not be rooted in selfish ambition, but in sacrificial usefulness. If your business, ministry, or platform does not serve people, it cannot attract sustainable favor.

God is not raising **spiritual celebrities**—He's raising **covenant servants** who lead through love, character, and contribution.

The power to get wealth is not somewhere in a distant land—it is already **inside you**. God has planted it in your spirit, wired it into your personality, and positioned it within your experiences.

Now, it's your turn.

- Develop it.
- Refine it.
- Activate it.
- Deploy it.

Don't wait until you have all the answers—move with the one you have. Don't wait for perfect conditions—start building with what's in your hand. Every great financial journey starts with a **step of obedience**.

The world doesn't need more wishful thinkers—we need more **value creators**. The Kingdom doesn't need more consumers—we need more **producers**. Your generation doesn't need more talkers—we need more **problem-solvers**.

You have the power. Now rise and use it.

God has already given you the power to get wealth. That power is hidden in your gifts, your obedience, your mindset, and your ability to create value. Your job is not to beg for money—it is to recognize, refine, and release what God has already placed within you.

You are not waiting on God. **He is waiting on you.**

CHAPTER 3

THE SPIRIT OF POVERTY

CHAPTER THREE

THE SPIRIT OF POVERTY

Identifying the Spirit Behind the Struggle

Poverty is not merely the absence of money—it is a **spirit, a mindset, and a stronghold**. It is a deeply rooted system designed to trap individuals, families, and even nations in cycles of limitation, despite being surrounded by opportunities.

You can receive money today and still remain poor in your thinking. You can land a great job and still make poverty-driven decisions. Why? Because poverty begins as a **spiritual stronghold** that influences how you think, plan, speak, and act.

The Spirit of Poverty

If you do not address the **spirit of poverty**, you will sabotage your own breakthroughs. You'll reject profitable relationships. You'll mismanage divine provision. You'll fear success. You'll despise prosperity teachings.

Poverty must be uprooted from the **spirit**, not just the wallet. The spirit of poverty whispers lies that feel like truth.

It tells you:

- "That's too much for someone like you."
- "You don't deserve a better life."
- "Stay in your lane—dreams like that are for others."
- "This is how it has always been in your family."

And over time, it **shrinks your vision**.

You stop praying boldly.

You stop planning aggressively.

You stop believing for more.

This spirit causes you to **normalize struggle**. You start settling for less, spiritualizing mediocrity, and defending scarcity as humility. You begin to think small, dream small, ask small, and expect small.

But poverty is not humility. And struggle is not sanctification.

God delights in seeing His children rise—not in pride, but in purpose and provision.

Poverty is often generational. It doesn't just pass through wallets—it passes through **belief systems, habits, and spiritual patterns**.

Maybe you come from a family where:

- No one owns land
- No one has built a lasting business
- No one finishes school
- No one marries successfully
- Everyone depends on someone else for survival

This isn't just coincidence—it is the **symptom of a system**. It's a cycle that must be identified, confronted, and broken through revelation, prayer, and new disciplines.

In Africa, these generational patterns often hide behind culture or "family history," but they are spiritual codes meant to be **decoded and dismantled**. And God has given you the power to rise and rewrite the story.

You may be the first in your family to break the poverty line—but by God's grace, you won't be the last.

Poverty's Patterns and Cycles

Deliverance from the spirit of poverty does not begin with laying on of hands—it begins with **renewing your mind**.

You can't rebuke poverty in prayer and yet keep agreeing with it in your thinking. You can't speak in tongues and still speak lack over your life. You can't fast for financial breakthrough and still operate with a poverty mentality.

Until your **thinking shifts**, your financial reality will remain the same.

Romans 12:2 says,

> *Be transformed by the renewing of your mind...*
>
> **Romans 12:2**

Not by money falling from the sky. Not by emotional excitement. **Transformation begins in the mind.**

God can open a financial door, but if your mindset is still chained to limitation, you'll walk through that door and still think small, spend poorly, or sabotage what He gave you.

Decoding Divine Wealth

To break free from poverty, your mind must align with abundance—even before your bank account does.

The poverty mindset is obsessed with **survival**, not legacy.

It constantly asks:

- "How do I get through today?"
- "What can I eat now?"
- "Where can I borrow money?"
- "How do I reduce my dreams to match my income?"

It's a mindset that fears **risk, investment, and innovation**. It discourages long-term thinking. It teaches people to despise tomorrow in pursuit of momentary relief today. But God is a generational thinker. He wants you to think like a builder, not just a consumer.

Instead of asking, *"What can I eat?"*, ask:

- "What can I plant?"
- "What can I create?"
- "What can I invest in?"
- "What system can I build that will outlive me?"

The Spirit of Poverty

If you want to break free from poverty, shift from short-term gratification to **eternal significance**. Start thinking like a **Kingdom builder**.

The spirit of poverty is **dangerously comfortable** with just getting by.

It teaches you to:

- Depend on others without seeking growth
- Excuse laziness with religious language
- Celebrate mediocrity as "contentment"
- Defend failure instead of confronting it
- Glorify suffering instead of learning from it

It will make you say things like:

- "At least I have something..."
- "We may be poor, but we're humble..."
- "God knows our hearts..."

While humility and contentment are virtues, they are never an excuse for **inaction, lack of vision, or systemic failure**.

In many families today, the spirit of poverty hides behind religious clichés. It convinces entire generations to stay in survival mode—avoiding excellence, rejecting discipline, and misquoting Scripture to stay stuck.

But God is not the author of mediocrity. He is the God of dominion, fruitfulness, and multiplication.

Confronting the Lies and Language of Lack

One of the clearest signs that the spirit of poverty is at work is when someone becomes **hostile toward wealth and those who possess it**.

This spirit criticizes people who succeed.

- It mocks those who dream big.
- It calls wealthy people greedy—without ever understanding their journey.
- It sees financial success as something to be feared or demonized.

Instead of asking, *"What can I learn from them?"* it asks, *"Who do they think they are?"*

This spirit thrives on bitterness, suspicion, and envy. It celebrates struggle and resents excellence.

The Spirit of Poverty

In some communities, the moment someone builds a house or buys a car, they're suspected of ritual money, fraud, or occult involvement. This toxic mindset prevents us from honoring hard work, learning financial principles, or raising the next generation of Kingdom financiers.

But the Word of God teaches us to **rejoice with those who rejoice** (Romans 12:15), not to slander them. If you criticize what you envy, you disqualify yourself from it.

Poverty is not just a condition—it is a **culture**. A culture that manifests in how people speak, dream, spend, and live.

It teaches you:

- To settle for less
- To silence your desires
- To avoid ambition in the name of humility
- To applaud crumbs and resist abundance
- To normalize borrowing, begging, and "managing" through life

In this culture, big dreams are ridiculed, financial literacy is scarce, and wealth creation is viewed with suspicion. Entire families, churches, and even communities can adopt this culture—passing it from one generation to the next like a family heirloom.

57

Decoding Divine Wealth

But Kingdom citizens must rise above this mentality. We must build a **culture of abundance**, where planning is celebrated, diligence is taught, giving is joyful, and creating wealth is not taboo—but testimony.

The only way to defeat the spirit of poverty is to **confront it with truth**—the truth of God's Word. Every lie it has planted in your mind must be uprooted and replaced:

- *"I can't succeed"* → "I can do all things through Christ…"
- *"This is just my portion in life"* → "I am blessed with every spiritual blessing…"
- *"I'll always struggle like my parents did"* → "I am the head and not the tail…"

You must renew your vocabulary. Stop speaking limitation. Start speaking abundance.

Stop rehearsing failure. Start declaring favor. Refuse to live small. Refuse to think small. Refuse to stay small.

You were not created to crawl—you were born to soar.

Rising in Identity and Declaring Your Freedom

To permanently break free from the spirit of poverty, you must receive a **revelation of your divine identity**.

- You are not ordinary.
- You are not cursed.
- You are not destined to struggle for survival all your life.

You are a **child of the King**—heaven's royalty on earth. You are seated with Christ in heavenly places (Ephesians 2:6). You carry the DNA of dominion, excellence, and abundance.

The enemy wants you to forget who you are so you'll settle for less than you were born to manifest. But God wants you to rise in the full confidence of your Kingdom heritage.

- Royalty doesn't beg.
- Kings don't grovel.
- Priests don't shrink.

Heirs don't apologize for their inheritance.

Start seeing yourself the way God sees you—and everything in your life will begin to shift.

Your tongue is a weapon. Use it to **prophesy your future**.

Declare with boldness:

- "I am blessed and highly favored."
- "I rise above every generational limitation."
- "I walk in divine abundance."
- "My hands are empowered to create wealth."
- "I think, speak, and act like someone sent to prosper."

As you speak, you rewire your thinking. As you declare, you break agreements with fear. As you affirm, you align your environment with your revelation.

- Speak life.
- Speak wealth.
- Speak destiny.
- And then—walk in it.

This is your moment to make a **spiritual and mental divorce from poverty**.

- You are not poor.
- You are not forgotten.
- You are not ordinary.

The Spirit of Poverty

You are:

- **Anointed to prosper**
- **Chosen to rise**
- **Empowered to break barriers**
- **Graced to shift generations**
- **Ordained to fund Kingdom purposes**

Refuse to settle.

Refuse to be small.

Refuse to be silent.

This is your time to rise. This is your time to break free. This is your time to walk in the power of divine wealth.

The spirit of poverty is more than a lack of cash—it's a demonic mindset designed to keep you small, silent, and stuck. It must be broken with the Word, uprooted from the heart, and replaced with a Kingdom identity.

You were born to build, to bless, to fund, and to flourish.

Your divine wealth journey begins where poverty ends—at the revelation of who you really are.

Decoding Divine Wealth

CHAPTER 4

KINGDOM PRINCIPLES FOR WEALTH

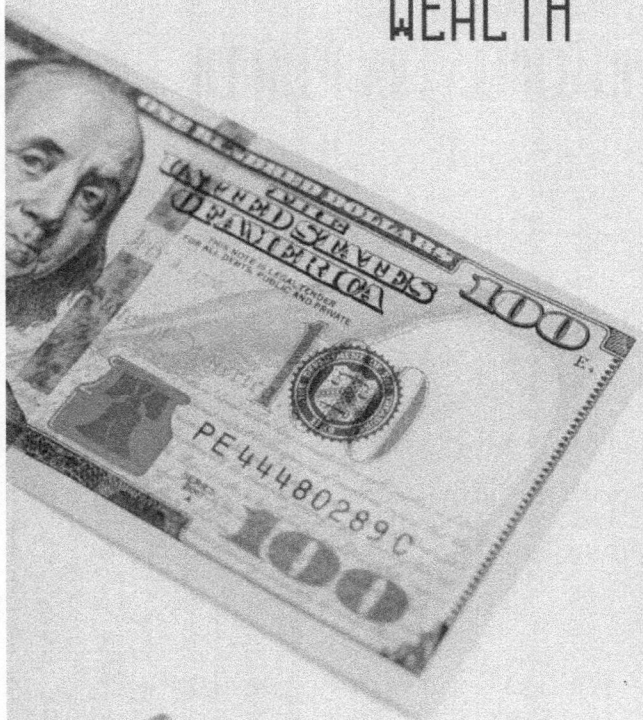

CHAPTER FOUR

KINGDOM PRINCIPLES FOR WEALTH

The Law of Giving—Unlocking Supernatural Flow

Wealth in the Kingdom of God is not built on luck, gambling, or manipulation—it is governed by **spiritual laws**. These laws are not emotional. They are not seasonal. They are not dependent on background, education, or nationality.

They are **consistent, universal,** and **non-negotiable**.

Kingdom Principles for Wealth

When you align with these laws, they work for you. When you ignore or violate them, you suffer loss—regardless of your love for God or the intensity of your prayer life.

In the natural world, laws like gravity work whether you believe in them or not. Similarly, Kingdom financial principles operate whether you're shouting "Amen" or not.

This is why two believers can serve the same God—one walking in abundance and the other stuck in lack—not because God is partial, but because one is **applying divine principles**, and the other is **ignoring them**.

If you want to enjoy lasting wealth, you must understand and apply the **Kingdom system of prosperity**.

The first major law of Kingdom wealth is the law of **giving**.

Luke 6:38 says,

> *Give, and it shall be given unto you; good measure, pressed down, shaken together, and running over...*

Luke 6:38

This is not about manipulation or emotional appeals for donations. It's a divine principle: **generosity unlocks divine circulation**.

When you release, you make room to receive. When you hoard, you halt the flow.

Giving in the Kingdom includes:

- Tithing to honor God as your Source
- Offering to worship Him with your substance
- Almsgiving to help the poor and needy
- Sowing seeds into fertile spiritual ground
- Supporting missions, widows, orphans, and Kingdom causes

This law is broader than church giving—it is a **lifestyle of open-handed living**.

In some parts of the world, where resources may be limited, the temptation is to withhold. But the Kingdom says: *"He who sows sparingly will also reap sparingly..."* (2 Corinthians 9:6). Giving doesn't subtract—it multiplies.

You don't wait until you have "more than enough" before you start giving. In the Kingdom, you **give your way into abundance**.

Isaac sowed in the time of famine—when others were hoarding—and reaped a hundredfold that same year

(Genesis 26:12). His act of obedience activated a supernatural harvest.

Many people say, *"I'll give when I have plenty."* But that's not faith—that's convenience. Faith says, *"Even in my lack, I will honor God and trust His system over my circumstance."*

Your seed may look small, but in God's hands, it becomes **a covenant trigger**. The widow at Zarephath gave Elijah her last meal and stepped into supernatural supply (1 Kings 17:8–16).

Don't despise your seed. Sow it in faith. Your future is hidden in what you're willing to release.

The Law of Work and the Grace to Build

Another unshakable law in the Kingdom system of wealth is the **law of work**.

Prayer is powerful. Fasting is essential. Prophecy is important. But none of these replaces the demand for **diligence**.

Deuteronomy 28:12 says God will bless **"all the work of your hands."** Not your daydreams. Not your declarations. Your **work**.

Many believers are deeply spiritual but financially stagnant—not because they lack grace, but because they lack **engagement**. They're waiting for breakthrough while refusing to build, learn, serve, or grow.

God does not bless idleness. Even Adam, in the perfection of Eden, was given the task to **"tend and keep"** the garden (Genesis 2:15). Jesus said,

My Father is always at His work to this very day, and I too am working.

John 5:17, (NIV)

Work is not a curse—it is a **channel of covenant release**.

Whether you are in ministry, business, education, agriculture, media, or government—your diligence is a prophetic key. Laziness is not anointed. Excellence is.

Joseph was gifted with **divine wisdom and prophetic insight**, but that was not all he had—**he worked**.

He managed Potiphar's estate with integrity and excellence. He served in prison with discipline and faithfulness. He interpreted Pharaoh's dream and followed it with a **national economic policy** that saved nations from famine.

God gave him power—but Joseph applied it through diligent work.

In the African context, many Christians are waiting for open doors they have not been prepared to walk through. They're waiting for elevation without education, for increase without effort, and for global relevance without local excellence.

Responsibility attracts resources. God will not finance what you refuse to manage.

If you want Kingdom wealth, then cultivate Kingdom **work ethic**. Let your name become synonymous with trust, diligence, excellence, and consistency.

One of the most ignored laws among spiritual people is the **law of planning**.

Yes, pray. But don't stop there.

Yes, believe. But follow your belief with blueprints.

Yes, fast. But let your fasting fuel clear goals, not just vague expectations.

God is a **God of patterns** and order. When He told Noah to build the ark, He gave him **dimensions**. When He called

Moses to build the tabernacle, He gave him **specifications**. Even Jesus said,

Which of you, intending to build a tower, does not sit down first and count the cost...

Luke 14:28

Planning is not carnal—it's covenantal. Document your vision. Write your financial targets. Break them into actionable steps. Budget with wisdom. Track your income and expenses.

As believers, we must learn to move beyond fire without form—beyond zeal without structure.

Your plan is the platform where your prayers land.

Planning, Honor, and the Path to Financial Maturity

The **law of honor** is one of the most spiritual—and most underestimated—keys to unlocking divine wealth.

Honor is not flattery. It is not blind loyalty. It is a **recognition of value**, a posture of the heart that opens doors and sustains favor.

If you:

- **Dishonor wealth**, you'll subconsciously repel it.
- **Dishonor mentors**, you'll block impartation.
- **Dishonor God**, you'll disconnect from the Source of all provision.

Proverbs 3:9 says,

Honor the Lord with your possessions, and with the firstfruits of all your increase.

Proverbs 3:9

Why? Because honor creates room for more. It is the bridge between where you are and where God is taking you.

In our world today, honor has been misused by some, but that does not invalidate its divine power. True honor is not forced—it flows from discernment. When you honor a vessel, a principle, or a divine instruction, you position yourself to **receive without resistance**.

Every great man carries a grace. What you **honor** will begin to flow in your direction.

Wealth does not answer to **sporadic inspiration**—it answers to **sustained consistency**.

Many people fail to prosper not because they lacked revelation, but because they lacked **endurance**. They sowed once and stopped. Planned once and gave up. Started a business and quit too soon. Dreamed big but lacked the discipline to keep building.

Galatians 6:9 says,

Let us not grow weary while doing good, for in due season we shall reap if we do not lose heart.

Galatians 6:9

The law of consistency says:

- Keep sowing—your harvest is cumulative.
- Keep showing up—your faithfulness builds credibility.
- Keep believing—even when nothing seems to be changing.
- Keep refining—your excellence will be rewarded.

In Africa, where economic instability often discourages long-term thinking, this principle is especially powerful. The storms may rage, but **keep standing**. Do not abort the process that's preparing your platform.

72

Your due season will not answer to **emotion**—it will respond to **consistency**.

These laws are not suggestions. They are not optional. They are not man-made concepts—they are **divine instructions** for dominion.

- Ignore them, and you will experience frustration.
- Mock them, and you will remain in cycles.
- Honor them, and you will rise—regardless of background, nationality, or opposition.

God is no respecter of persons, but He is a respecter of principles.

If you do what Abraham did, you can walk in what Abraham walked in. If you obey like Joseph, you can prosper like Joseph.

Kingdom wealth is predictable—it follows **laws**, not luck.

Obedience in Action—From Revelation to Manifestation

The power of Kingdom wealth is not activated by knowledge alone—it is unlocked through **obedience**.

James 1:22 tells us,

But be doers of the word, and not hearers only, deceiving yourselves.

James 1:22

Don't just shout *Amen* during a sermon or write notes in your journal—**do the Word**.

- Start giving consistently.
- Start working diligently.
- Start planning intentionally.
- Start honoring strategically.
- Start believing persistently.

The blessing is in the **doing**. It is your alignment with God's principles that positions you for God's provision.

Many believers remain poor—not because they weren't taught—but because they refused to act. Heaven is not moved by information. Heaven responds to **application**.

You cannot prosper by accident—you prosper by action.

Start small, but **start now**.

Don't wait until everything lines up. Don't delay until conditions are perfect. Don't keep saying, *"One day…"*—make today **Day One**.

- Sow from what you have, not what you hope for.
- Plan with the little in your hands—it will multiply.
- Work with excellence, even when no one is watching.
- Honor God where you are, and He will lift you higher.

Ecclesiastes 11:4 says,

He who observes the wind will not sow, and he who regards the clouds will not reap.

Ecclesiastes 11:4

If you keep postponing, you will keep losing ground. Your **obedience today** determines your **increase tomorrow**.

God doesn't need you to be perfect—He needs you to be **responsive**.

These Kingdom principles are not abstract theories—they are **tested, proven, and powerful**.

I am not sharing motivational phrases. I am sharing truth that I've walked through, lived out, and watched transform others.

I've seen poverty broken. I've watched doors open. I've witnessed favor flow. And it all began when I chose to **align with God's financial system**.

If it worked for Abraham, Joseph, Ruth, David, and countless others—it can work for you.

You are not too late. You are not too far behind. You are not too unqualified.

Just begin. Align. Obey. Sow. Work. Honor. Persist!

And watch God move.

Wealth in the Kingdom is governed by divine laws—giving, working, planning, honoring, and staying consistent. These laws are not emotional—they are eternal. If you align with them, they will elevate you.

Start where you are. Use what you have. Honor what God has revealed. And your journey into divine wealth will not just begin—it will flourish.

CHAPTER 5

BREAKING FINANCIAL LIMITATIONS

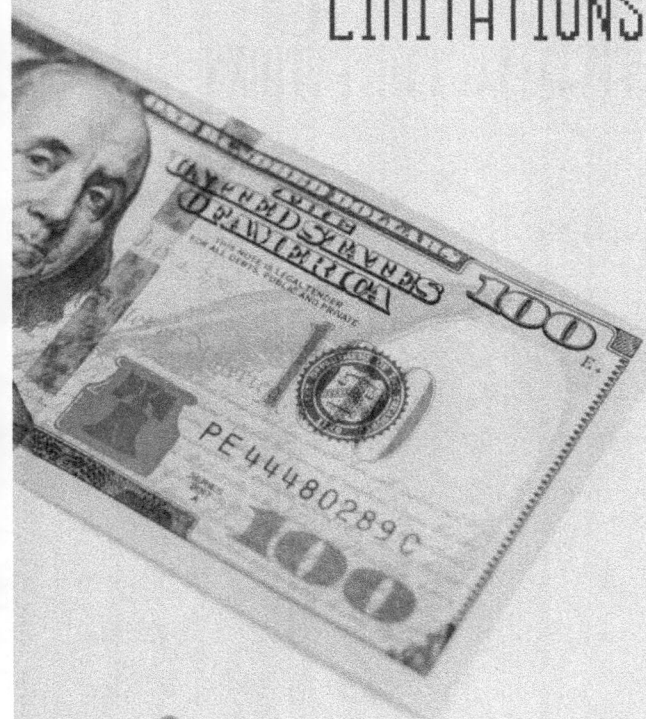

CHAPTER FIVE

BREAKING FINANCIAL LIMITATIONS

Discerning Invisible Barriers to Financial Progress

There are moments when you're doing all the right things—working hard, giving faithfully, planning diligently, praying earnestly—and yet, you feel **stuck**.

It's as though you're hitting an invisible wall. You make money, but it slips through your fingers. Doors open briefly, then close unexpectedly. Every progress feels like a battle. What you're facing is not just economic—it's **spiritual**.

That's what we call a **financial limitation**—a hidden barrier designed to **frustrate your fruitfulness**.

These limitations are not always visible to the natural eye, but they're real. They operate like invisible ceilings, keeping people from rising no matter how gifted or committed they are. Until these are identified and broken, financial progress will always feel like a struggle.

Financial limitations often have **multiple sources**—and they can be deeply layered.

They may come through:

- **Generational curses**: Patterns of lack, debt, or collapse running through family lines
- **Wrong mindsets**: Deeply embedded beliefs that reject abundance and normalize scarcity
- **Demonic opposition**: Forces that resist breakthrough through manipulation, delay, or destruction
- **Poor financial decisions**: Repeated mistakes, mismanagement, or financial ignorance

Sometimes, it's not one thing—it's a combination.

You might be praying, but also making unwise choices. Or giving, but thinking destructively. Or working hard, but dealing with a curse of stagnation that runs through your bloodline.

To walk in total freedom, you must **discern every layer**, then engage with prayer, wisdom, and prophetic action. Victory begins with **revelation**. You cannot conquer what you haven't discerned. Many people fight in the dark—swinging aimlessly at symptoms while the real root remains untouched.

Ask the Holy Spirit:

- "Where did this financial pattern begin?"
- "Is there something I'm not seeing?"
- "What spiritual laws have I violated?"
- "What do I need to repent of, renounce, or correct?"

The Holy Spirit is your divine diagnostic tool. He doesn't just reveal problems—He reveals **patterns**, and then shows you the **principles** to break them.

Your breakthrough will not just come from shouting in prayer—it will come from **spiritual intelligence** and targeted action.

Engaging Spiritual Warfare and Practical Wisdom

Some financial limitations are rooted in **covenants**—whether spoken, unspoken, intentional, or inherited.

Perhaps a family member entered into a **demonic agreement** or made a **vow of poverty**, especially in religious or traditional settings. These covenants, though forgotten or ignored, remain spiritually binding until **broken by revelation and authority**.

But it's not just ancestral covenants. Many believers make **inner vows** without realizing it:

- "I'll never be rich; money changes people."
- "I'd rather be poor and holy."
- "We've never had anything in this family—and I'm okay with that."
- "I don't need much—just enough to survive."

These are not harmless thoughts. They are **word-based covenants** that program your spirit for limitation. You cannot rise beyond the boundaries your own mouth has created.

Proverbs 6:2 says,

81

You are snared by the words of your mouth...

Proverbs 6:2

To break free, you must **renounce wrong covenants** and replace them with covenant truth.

There are certain barriers that will not bow to casual prayers or lukewarm faith. They require **intense spiritual warfare, fasting**, and **targeted declarations**.

Jesus said in Matthew 17:21 (NKJV),

However, this kind does not go out except by prayer and fasting.

Matthew 17:21 (NKJV)

Fasting sharpens your spiritual sensitivity.

Prayer activates angelic assistance.

Declarations release divine authority.

You must stand in your authority as a covenant child of God and declare:

- "Every curse of financial stagnation in my bloodline is broken!"

- "I renounce every vow, agreement, or word that opposes my prosperity!"
- "I align with the covenant of Abraham—blessed to be a blessing!"
- "No limitation can survive the presence of the Living God!"

This is not hype—this is spiritual enforcement. If you don't contend for your freedom, the enemy will continue to exploit ignorance and inaction.

Spiritual warfare without **practical wisdom** leads to frustration.

Once you've prayed, fasted, and declared, it's time to make **new decisions**. Break cycles. Shift habits. Grow in **financial intelligence**.

Start by:

- Tracking your income and expenses
- Creating a realistic budget
- Eliminating unnecessary debt
- Saving consistently, even if it's small
- Investing in knowledge—books, trainings, mentorship

- Practicing delayed gratification

In many developing contexts, bad financial habits are often spiritualized. People rebuke the devourer in prayer but welcome him through impulsive spending.

God is not just looking for people who **pray well**—He's looking for people who **manage well**. You must match your prayer altar with personal discipline.

Shifting Environments, Associations, and Mindsets

One of the most overlooked sources of financial limitation is your **circle of influence**. The people you surround yourself with either:

- **Feed your future** or drain your destiny
- Inspire growth or normalize stagnation
- Celebrate discipline or mock it
- Push you to rise or pull you back into complacency

Proverbs 13:20 says,

He who walks with wise men will be wise, but the companion of fools will be destroyed.

Proverbs 13:20

You can't walk in abundance while moving with those who idolize mediocrity. You can't pursue vision while staying loyal to friends who distract you from purpose.

If your inner circle mocks your savings habit, belittles your goals, or promotes careless spending—you're sabotaging your financial growth.

Disconnection is often a prerequisite for elevation.

Let some people go so your destiny can grow.

Environment is prophetic. It shapes your perception, limits, and expectations.

Sometimes, financial limitations are sustained because you're surrounded by **small thinking**, low standards, or oppressive structures—physically, emotionally, or even spiritually.

Elevation often begins with **exposure**.

- Travel if you can, even to nearby cities or environments that challenge your thinking
- Read books that expand your mindset
- Follow mentors who provoke excellence

- Visit places that make you dream again
- Sit in rooms that stretch your faith

You may not be able to move physically yet, but you can move **mentally**. Break out of the prison of "just enough." Train your mind to see more, believe more, expect more.

Your location doesn't have to define your elevation—unless you allow it.

Breaking financial limitations is not a **one-time prayer point**—it's a **lifestyle of growth**.

It's a journey of:

- Continuous learning
- Daily surrender
- Radical obedience
- Intentional discipline
- Progressive mindset shifts

There may be instant breakthroughs, but lasting freedom comes through **daily alignment with Kingdom truth**.

Every new level of wealth will test your maturity. Every elevation will require an upgrade in thinking, stewardship, and humility.

Don't relax after the first breakthrough. Don't settle when small victories come. Keep growing. Keep learning. Keep pressing.

The enemy will try to reintroduce old patterns—**don't fall for them**. You've come too far to go back.

Walking Boldly into Your Wealthy Place

Let this truth echo in your spirit: **You are not cursed. You are not forgotten. You are not destined for perpetual struggle.**

You are a **covenant child of God**. You carry the **blessing of Abraham** (Galatians 3:14). You are designed to **prosper, multiply, and dominate** in your assignment.

You are seated in heavenly places, operating from a position of spiritual authority.

Poverty is not your inheritance. Struggle is not your portion. Limitations are not your legacy.

You may come from a family of lack, but you are called to break that cycle and start a new lineage—one of wealth, wisdom, impact, and Kingdom relevance.

It's time to use your mouth as a **weapon of deliverance**.

Declare:

- "I break every invisible barrier to my financial progress!"
- "I cancel every generational pattern of lack and limitation!"
- "I rise into the wealthy place prepared for me by God!"
- "I am blessed, fruitful, and established in Kingdom abundance!"
- "I think like a king, walk like a builder, and sow like a covenant man!"
- "I break free from fear, stagnation, and delay. My season of overflow has come!"

You were not created to blend in—you were created to **break through**.

- Refuse to settle in average.

- Refuse to make peace with smallness.
- Refuse to normalize limitation.

You have a divine mandate to **rise**, to **prosper**, and to **fund the Kingdom agenda** on earth.

Your **wealthy place** is not a fantasy—it is **prophetic**, **scriptural**, and **attainable**.

Psalm 66:12 says, *"You brought us out to rich fulfillment."* Another version calls it a **"wealthy place."**

It exists. It has your name on it. But you must **contend** for it.

- Fight in prayer
- Fast with purpose
- Sow sacrificially
- Plan intentionally
- Work diligently
- Declare prophetically
- Walk faithfully

This is not just about money—it's about **divine positioning**, **Kingdom relevance**, and **generational transformation**.

You're not just called to escape poverty. You're called to **redefine prosperity**—the kind that glorifies God, lifts others, and leaves a legacy.

Financial limitations are real—but they are not permanent. They are breakable. They respond to revelation, repentance, spiritual warfare, and practical wisdom.

You are anointed to prosper. Chosen to rise. Empowered to build.

Now—step into your wealthy place.

CHAPTER 6

BUILDING FINANCIAL
STRUCTURES THAT LAST

CHAPTER SIX

BUILDING FINANCIAL STRUCTURES THAT LAST

Preparing for Prosperity Through Order

Desiring wealth is one thing—**sustaining it is another**. Many believers cry out for financial breakthrough, but few are prepared with the **structures necessary to manage increase**.

The truth is, God is not just interested in putting money in your hands. He wants to give you **wisdom, systems, and strategies** to ensure that money doesn't pass through you— it grows through you.

Why? Because **wealth without structure is temporary**.

- Without structure, increase becomes stress.

- Without structure, blessings become burdens.

- Without structure, prosperity becomes a trap.

This is why Proverbs 24:3–4 (NLT) says,

A house is built by wisdom and becomes strong through good sense. Through knowledge its rooms are filled with all sorts of precious riches and valuables.

Proverbs 24:3-4 (NLT)

Wisdom builds wealth. But structure sustains it.

Financial structure is about establishing **order** in your financial life.

It means:

- You have a **budget**: a clear picture of income and expenses

- You have a **savings plan**: emergency and long-term reserves

- You have a **giving strategy**: consistent tithing, offerings, and generosity

- You have an **investment path**: putting money to work

- You **track your money** and know where every naira, dollar, or cedi is going

Structure is not just for rich people—it's how they became rich.

In many African settings, people resist financial planning, calling it "Western thinking" or "too technical." But structure is **biblical**, and it's essential for anyone who wants to move from paycheck to overflow.

Even in spiritual matters, God works through order. Wealth responds to **stewardship**, not just shouting "Amen."

Here's a principle that changes everything: **God will not bless beyond your ability to manage.**

Luke 16:10 says,

> *He who is faithful in what is least is faithful also in much...*
>
> **Luke 16:10**

If you:

- Waste the little, you disqualify yourself from the much
- Mismanage small income, you close the door to larger streams

- Complain about your current state, instead of stewarding it—you delay your own elevation

God isn't withholding because He's mean. He's waiting for **capacity**.

Many people don't need more money—they need more **management skills**. They're praying for financial miracles while ignoring the principles of order, record-keeping, discipline, and accountability.

God is not just looking for containers—He's looking for systems that can handle and multiply His blessing.

Structuring Your Finances with Purpose and Discipline

One of the most powerful steps you can take toward lasting wealth is to **track your money**—faithfully, honestly, and consistently.

Yes, pray. Yes, give. But also, **write things down**.

- Know exactly what comes in (your income)
- Know exactly what goes out (your expenses)
- Know where your money is going—not just where you wish it went

95

- Know what you're spending impulsively and what's yielding return

The truth is, most people don't have a money problem—they have a management problem.

You cannot master what you don't measure. You cannot steward what you don't study.

In certain communities, we often leave money matters to chance or guesswork. But divine wealth answers to **clarity, not confusion**. Even Jesus said, *"Gather the fragments, that nothing be lost."* (John 6:12)

A financially structured life is not about obsession—it's about **obedience and wisdom.**

Contrary to popular belief, budgeting is not bondage—it is freedom.

It's not about restriction—it's about **direction**. It's not about saying "no" to life—it's about saying "yes" to purpose.

A budget is a prophetic map. It allows you to:

- Take control of your financial flow

- Allocate resources according to your values
- Avoid unnecessary pressure
- Prepare for opportunities in advance

Without a budget, your money becomes an unruly servant. With a budget, it becomes a faithful steward. In many homes, financial stress is not due to insufficient income— it's due to disorganized spending.

If you're serious about wealth, start budgeting like your destiny depends on it—because it does. A Kingdom financial structure is incomplete **without God at the center**.

Don't tithe from what is left—**tithe from the top**. Don't give as an afterthought—**make generosity a line item in your budget**.

Don't make God chase you for what already belongs to Him—**honor Him first**.

Proverbs 3:9–10 says,

Honor the Lord with your wealth, with the firstfruits of all your crops; then your barns will be filled to overflowing.

Proverbs 3:9–10

When you place God first in your finances:

- You invite Him into your stewardship
- You align your heart with Kingdom priorities
- You protect yourself from greed and idolatry

Make giving your **first instinct**, not your last resort.

Let your structure **prophesy your faith**. Let your spreadsheet preach your trust in God. Let your bank statements testify that you are not owned by money—you steward it for the glory of God.

Saving, Investing, and Growing with Mentorship

Saving is not doubt—it is wisdom.

In Genesis 41, Joseph received a divine strategy to save Egypt: store grain during seven years of plenty to prepare for the seven years of famine. That decision didn't just preserve a nation—it preserved a **prophetic lineage**.

Saving is:

- Honoring the future
- Preparing for unpredictability
- Creating stability

- Protecting purpose

Some believers wrongly see saving as fear or mistrust. But saving is not denying God—it's applying His principles.

Proverbs 21:20 (NLT) says,

The wise have wealth and luxury, but fools spend whatever they get.
Proverbs 21:20 (NLT)

A structured financial life includes:

- Emergency funds (for life's unexpected turns)
- Reserve funds (for business or ministry opportunities)
- Legacy funds (for children and future generations)

Don't just spend everything because it's in your account. Let your **present discipline secure your future destiny**.

Investment is where the journey from **income to wealth** truly begins. Working earns you a living—but **investing builds your legacy**.

Earning is active—investing creates passive multiplication. When you invest wisely, your money starts working even when you're sleeping.

Ecclesiastes 11:2 says,

Decoding Divine Wealth

Invest in seven ventures, yes, in eight; you do not know what disaster may come upon the land.

Ecclesiastes 11:2

But here's the key: **invest with knowledge**.

- Study investment principles
- Understand risk and reward
- Ask questions
- Seek counsel from those who have results
- Start small if you must, but **start smart**

In Africa and other emerging economies, many people fall prey to "get-rich-quick" schemes because they were never taught **patient, principled investing**.

God wants your money to grow, not just flow. But growth takes time, strategy, and stewardship. You were never meant to **build financial systems in isolation**.

Lone wolves struggle longer. But those who walk with the wise **accelerate**.

Proverbs 15:22 says,

Plans fail for lack of counsel, but with many advisers they succeed.

Proverbs 15:22

If you're serious about building financial structures that last:

- **Find financial mentors** who walk in what you desire
- **Join learning communities** that challenge your thinking
- **Submit your plan for review**—don't be afraid of correction
- **Stay accountable** so your growth isn't based on emotion, but wisdom

In our culture, people sometimes hide their financial struggles out of pride. But silence can keep you stuck. Wealth flows where **humility meets mentorship**.

You don't need to know everything—you just need to **ask the right people** and apply what they share.

Structuring for Generational Wealth and Kingdom Impact

Many mistake **structure** for self-reliance, but in truth, structure is not the absence of faith—it is the **evidence of faith**.

Noah built an ark *before* it rained.

Elisha told the widow to gather vessels *before* the oil flowed. Jesus told the crowd to sit in groups *before* the miracle of multiplication.

God honors **preparation**. He fills what you build. He expands what you steward. He multiplies what you manage.

If you build systems for income, saving, giving, and growth—God will entrust you with increase. He's not looking for emotional givers alone—He's looking for **wise builders**.

Psalm 127:1 says,

> *Unless the Lord builds the house, they labor in vain who build it.*
>
> **Psalm 127:1**

But the Lord cannot build what you refuse to start. If you build wisely, God will bless **abundantly**. Start where you are. Don't wait for a financial windfall before you build structure.

- **Organize your finances** today
- **Create a budget** that aligns with your purpose

- **Plan your generosity** as a lifestyle, not a reaction
- **Commit to savings**, even if it's modest
- **Track your spending** and find the leaks
- **Pray for wisdom**, and then apply it with diligence

God doesn't multiply chaos. He blesses **order**.

You don't build structure after abundance—you build it to **invite abundance**. You don't wait until you have more—you steward what's in your hand now as proof you're ready for more.

The kind of wealth God wants to release into your life is not just survival money—it's **generational, transformational, and missional**.

It's for:

- Your **children's children**
- The **Kingdom projects** He will entrust to you
- The **souls**, schools, and systems you are called to impact
- The **legacy** that will outlive your name

So build like someone who is not just saving money—but **shaping nations**.

Don't build for the weekend. Build for the **next 100 years**. Don't just prepare for a season. Prepare for a **spiritual legacy**.

Wealth without structure collapses. But wealth with Kingdom structure endures and multiplies across generations.

God wants to bless you financially—but He's looking for **structures** that can sustain increase.

Build with wisdom. Track your income. Plan your giving. Budget with vision. Save intentionally. Invest carefully. Learn continuously.

Then watch God fill what you've built—with **overflow, excellence, and endurance**.

CHAPTER 7

STREAMS OF INCOME AND KINGDOM EXPANSION

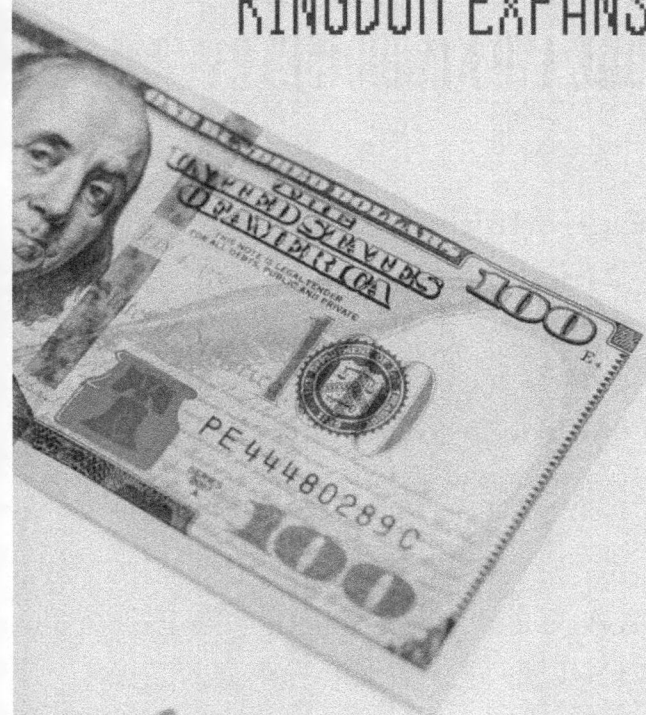

CHAPTER SEVEN

STREAMS OF INCOME AND KINGDOM EXPANSION

The Eden Pattern—Multiplying Streams of Increase

One of the greatest financial mistakes among believers is **depending on only one source of income**. It is risky, limiting, and not aligned with the model of divine abundance.

From the beginning, God gave us a pattern in the Garden of Eden. Genesis 2:10–14 tells us the garden was watered by **four rivers**, not one. Each river had a name, a direction, and wealth attached to it—gold, bdellium, and onyx stone were mentioned.

106

Streams of Income and Kingdom Expansion

Why would God place multiple rivers in one garden?

Because **divine prosperity is never one-dimensional**. He doesn't want you living in survival mode, waiting for salary day. He wants you walking in wisdom, building systems, and multiplying streams—each one releasing increase and expanding your Kingdom impact.

God can—and does—bless jobs. Your career is a valid and honorable source of income.

But don't stop there. Don't bury your other gifts while clinging to one paycheck.

- Are you good at teaching? Start a coaching class.
- Can you bake? Launch a weekend bakery.
- Do you write well? Offer editing or content services.
- Do you have farming knowledge? Start small and grow.

Your job is a seedbed—but your other skills, ideas, and relationships are potential **rivers**.

Ecclesiastes 11:6 (NIV) says,

Sow your seed in the morning, and at evening let your hands not be idle, for you do not know which will succeed...

Ecclesiastes 11:6 (NIV)

In our world today, economic uncertainty demands financial agility. Kingdom citizens should be the most innovative, disciplined, and solution-driven individuals on earth.

Don't just pray for overflow—**create systems for it.**

Having multiple income streams gives you **stability, security, and spiritual leverage**.

- It helps you stay afloat during unexpected seasons.
- It gives you options—so you don't have to compromise values to survive.
- It positions you to become a **greater blessing**.

Deuteronomy 15:6 says,

> *You shall lend to many nations, but you shall not borrow.*

Deuteronomy 15:6

You can't be a lender if you're always waiting for your salary to drop. You can't be a Kingdom financier if you're stuck in paycheck-to-paycheck cycles. **Multiple streams make you resilient.** They break the back of dependency.

God didn't call you to survive—He called you to **empower nations**.

Focus, Discernment, and Excellence in Every Stream

While multiple streams of income are biblical and beneficial, you must avoid the trap of **distraction masquerading as diversification**.

- Not every business idea is divine.
- Not every "opportunity" is ordained.
- Not every stream is your assignment.

What begins as a good venture can become a burden if it pulls you away from purpose.

Proverbs 4:25–27 (NIV) says,

Let your eyes look straight ahead; fix your gaze directly before you... do not swerve to the right or the left.

Proverbs 4:25–27 (NIV)

You don't need **ten unfinished projects**. You need **a few focused streams**, built with excellence, faith, and integrity.

Before launching a new venture:

- Pray for divine clarity
- Assess your current capacity
- Seek wise counsel
- Consider its alignment with your long-term Kingdom assignment

Distraction spreads you thin. Focus multiplies your impact. Not all income streams are created equal. Some are **seasonal blessings**, while others are **foundational lifelines**.

- A seasonal stream might meet a need for a short time but isn't designed for the long haul
- A foundational stream sustains you consistently and aligns with your long-term call and capacity

Learn to **discern the difference**.

Too many people abandon the **main thing** for something trendy—only to lose both. Don't sacrifice your stable foundation for a fleeting thrill.

Ecclesiastes 3:1 reminds us: *"To everything there is a season…"*

When God gives you a stream, ask:

- Is this temporary or long-term?

- Is this meant to support or become a core structure?
- Is this pulling me toward purpose—or away from it?

Your discernment determines your durability.

Whether you're a coach, caterer, consultant, craftsman, or content creator—whatever stream God gives you, **pursue it with excellence.**

- Package your offering well
- Deliver on your promises
- Communicate clearly
- Solve real problems
- Reflect Kingdom standards in everything you do

Colossians 3:23 says,

> *Whatever you do, do it heartily, as to the Lord and not to men.*
>
> **Colossians 3:23**

In a noisy world full of shortcuts and sloppy service, your **excellence will be your evangelism**.

Don't just be another voice in the crowd—be a **solution with distinction**. God is not glorified by mediocrity. He is glorified when your business, service, or craft carries the fragrance of purpose and the fingerprint of Heaven.

Purpose-Driven Profit and the Test of Prosperity

The reason God gives you the **power to create wealth** is not so you can consume endlessly—it is so you can **advance His Kingdom** on the earth.

Wealth is a **tool**, not a trophy. It is a **means**, not the end. Your income is meant to fund **vision**, and your profit is meant to **empower purpose**.

Deuteronomy 8:18 says,

But remember the Lord your God, for it is He who gives you power to get wealth, that He may establish His covenant...

Deuteronomy 8:18

So ask yourself:

- Is my income aligned with my assignment?
- Is my profit serving people or just self?
- Am I building platforms that elevate Christ or just elevate me?

When money becomes a servant of the mission, you will find **supernatural multiplication and favor**.

Kingdom expansion requires Kingdom financiers.

As God increases your streams, He's not just blessing you—He's **trusting you**. With every new flow comes a divine invitation: *"Will you use this to build My Kingdom?"*

Use your resources to:

- Support missions and soul-winning campaigns
- Fund churches, conferences, and media outreach
- Sponsor education, healthcare, and humanitarian initiatives
- Empower the next generation of leaders, authors, and revivalists

You were never meant to be a **vault**—you were called to be a **vessel**. God pours into those who pour out.

Proverbs 11:25 says,

The generous will prosper; those who refresh others will themselves be refreshed.

Proverbs 11:25

Kingdom wealth is **impact-driven**. It's not just about cash flow—it's about **purpose flow**.

Decoding Divine Wealth

Wealth is not just a blessing—it is a **test**. And not everyone passes.

As God expands your streams, **stay grounded**. Let your heart remain low, even when your accounts rise high.

- Don't let money change your honor for God.
- Don't let profit replace your posture in prayer.
- Don't let increase reduce your intimacy.
- Don't let success create spiritual pride.

1 Timothy 6:17 says,

Command those who are rich... not to be arrogant nor to put their hope in wealth, which is so uncertain, but to put their hope in God...

1 Timothy 6:17

God is watching to see:

- Will you still worship when you can buy anything you want?
- Will you still give when you feel like you've "made it"?
- Will you still obey when you're not desperate?

True Kingdom wealth flows from humility and flows back into purpose.

Start with What You Have and Submit It to God

The most powerful streams often begin with **what you already have**.

You may not have a large bank account, but you have:

- **Ideas** that solve real problems
- **Skills** developed over time
- **Relationships** that open doors
- **Opportunities** that others are overlooking
- **Time** that you can invest wisely

Don't wait for a "miracle investor" or a mysterious breakthrough—**start moving**.

When God asked Moses what he had in his hand, it was just a staff. But that staff, submitted in faith, became a **tool of signs and wonders**.

What's in your hand today?

Start small, but start now. God breathes on movement, not on passivity. As you act, the grace for expansion will meet you on the journey.

Before you run with your plans, **submit your streams to the Stream-Giver**.

- **Dedicate your businesses, side hustles, and creative ventures to God**
- Invite Him into every boardroom, brainstorm, and transaction
- Ask Him for divine direction, insight, and acceleration

Isaiah 45:3 says,

I will give you the treasures of darkness and hidden riches of secret places...

Isaiah 45:3

Only God knows where the gold is buried. He knows which stream carries longevity, which client holds your next season, which door leads to generational impact.

So don't just ask Him to bless your hustle—ask Him to **breathe on your blueprint**.

Streams of Income and Kingdom Expansion

Let your streams be **Spirit-led**, not stress-led.

Let every income stream flowing through your life become an **altar of worship** and a **channel of Kingdom advancement**.

- Let your streams **reflect excellence**, not mediocrity
- Let your products and services **carry integrity** and transformation
- Let your profits **empower vision**, not just comfort
- Let your business systems **model stewardship and generosity**
- Let your impact **outlive your income**

You were not just born to earn—you were born to **overflow**. Not just to have streams, but to become a **fountain of refreshing for others**.

Not just to multiply income, but to **multiply influence and inheritance**. As your streams flow, may they carry healing, help, and **Heaven's fragrance** everywhere they go.

You were never designed to rely on a single stream. Like the rivers in Eden, God has positioned multiple flows around you—gifts, ideas, relationships, insights, and opportunities.

Pursue them with prayer. Build them with purpose. Offer them with excellence.

Let your income become impact. Let your streams serve the King.

CHAPTER 8

THE POWER OF FINANCIAL VISION

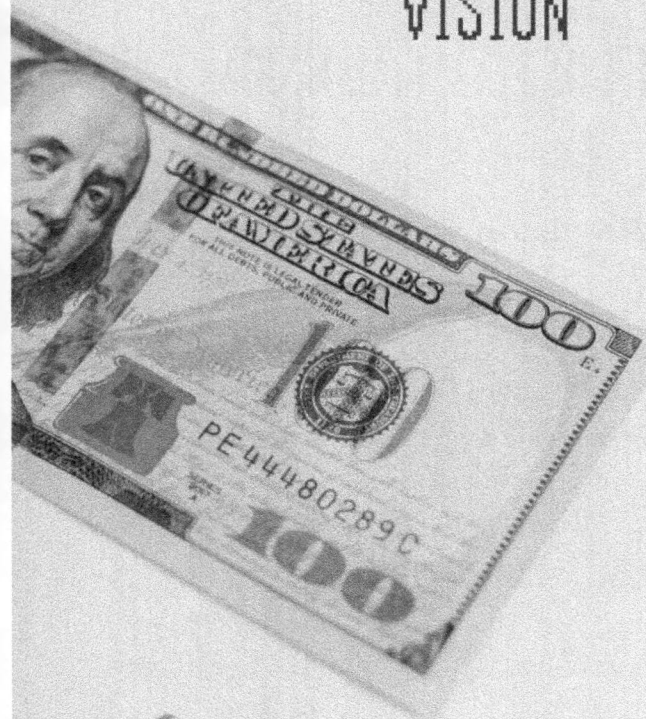

CHAPTER EIGHT

THE POWER OF FINANCIAL VISION

Aligning Provision with Purpose

Without a **clear financial vision**, even divine provision can be mismanaged. Vision gives direction. It tells your money where to go, how to grow, and why it even matters.

Proverbs 29:18 says, *"Where there is no vision, the people perish..."*—and that includes financial destiny.

- Without vision, you'll chase trends instead of purpose
- Without vision, you'll confuse distractions for opportunities
- Without vision, you'll waste miracles on survival

The Power of Financial Vision

- Without vision, your finances will drift instead of drive

Many people are praying for more money, but God is asking: *"What will you do with what I've already given?"*

Vision is what qualifies you for more.

Financial vision is not just about budgets and spreadsheets—it's about **purposeful imagination**.

- What do you want to build with your wealth?
- Who are you called to support?
- What causes burn in your spirit?
- What kind of legacy do you want to leave behind?

Financial vision is the **why** behind the wealth.

When money flows without mission, it leads to **mismanagement** and often pride. But when money is tied to a God-given vision, it becomes **Kingdom ammunition**.

You're not just here to make a living—you're here to make a **difference**. Prayer sets the atmosphere—but **planning builds the altar** where the blessing rests.

Habakkuk 2:2 says,

Decoding Divine Wealth

Write the vision, and make it plain...

Habakkuk 2:2

Don't just pray for abundance—**plan for it.**

- Create **giving goals**—what ministries or missions will you support?
- Create **saving goals**—what emergencies or expansions are you preparing for?
- Set **business targets**—what income levels, client milestones, or product launches are you aiming for?
- Map out **investment targets**—what vehicles will grow your money wisely?

Your vision doesn't have to be big at first—but it must be **clear**. A vague vision produces a vague result. A clear vision attracts clear favor.

From Survival to Significance

Your financial vision must be **bigger than your bills** and **deeper than your needs**.

Survival is not vision. Paying rent is not destiny. Buying groceries is not legacy.

122

The Power of Financial Vision

If your financial prayers and plans are only centered on **getting by**, you'll never break into **significance**.

God wants you to:

- Dream **beyond your immediate needs**
- See yourself as a **Kingdom contributor**, not just a consumer
- Think in terms of **impact**, **legacy**, and **generational relevance**

Ephesians 3:20 reminds us that God is *"able to do exceedingly abundantly above all we ask or think..."* But what are you thinking? What are you seeing?

If your mind is stuck in survival, your finances will stay there too. Vision does more than inspire you—it **disciplines you**.

When your financial life is guided by a clear purpose:

- You'll **say no** to unnecessary spending
- You'll **delay gratification** because legacy is more important than luxury
- You'll **ignore distractions** and stay committed to the bigger picture
- You'll **press forward** even when growth feels slow

Proverbs 25:28 says,

Whoever has no rule over his own spirit is like a city broken down, without walls.

Proverbs 25:28

Vision builds those walls. It protects your focus, filters your options, and preserves your energy. Without vision, every sale looks like a need. Every opportunity looks like a calling. Every expense feels justified. But when you carry a **clear Kingdom financial vision**, you spend, save, give, and build with holy intentionality.

There will be moments when the journey feels slow, the effort feels invisible, and the results seem far off. In those moments, **vision becomes your fuel**.

Vision speaks to your spirit and says:

- "This sacrifice is worth it."
- "You're building something that eyes have not seen."
- "Your obedience today is laying the foundation for generations."
- "Keep moving—your wealthy place is ahead."

Galatians 6:9 says,

124

Let us not become weary in doing good, for at the proper time we will reap a harvest if we do not give up.

Galatians 6:9

When motivation fades, vision takes over. When results delay, vision endures. When others laugh or misunderstand, vision keeps you anchored.

- Don't just work hard—**see clearly.**
- Don't just sow seeds—**see harvests.**
- Don't just count coins—**count impact.**

God-Given Blueprints and the Written Plan

One of the clearest indicators that you're walking with God financially is this: **you carry vision.**

Why? Because **God Himself is a visionary.**

He never acts randomly. He sees the end from the beginning (Isaiah 46:10). Everything He does flows from a **blueprint, a purpose, and a prophetic agenda.**

Throughout Scripture:

- God gave **Abraham** a vision of nations and inheritance

- He gave **Joseph** dreams of rulership and economic preservation
- He gave **Moses** a detailed pattern for building the tabernacle
- He gave **David** blueprints for the temple, even though Solomon would build it
- He gave **Jesus** a vision that endured the cross for the joy set before Him (Hebrews 12:2)

If God leads by vision, then you must manage your money by **revelation, not reaction**.

Stop guessing. Stop drifting. **Start building what Heaven has shown you.** Don't just create goals—**seek a financial blueprint from Heaven.**

Ask God in prayer:

- "What are You calling me to build?"
- "Who am I called to serve through my wealth?"
- "What streams do You want me to activate?"
- "How should I structure my financial life to reflect divine purpose?"

The Power of Financial Vision

When your financial vision is **downloaded from the Spirit**, it comes with:

- **Heaven's backing**
- **Unusual favor**
- **Supernatural provision**
- **Divine protection**

Isaiah 48:17 says,

I am the Lord your God, who teaches you to profit, who leads you in the way you should go.

Isaiah 48:17

When you receive a financial blueprint from God, **your giving becomes prophetic**, your saving becomes strategic, and your business becomes ministry.

Your financial vision should not stay in your head—it must be **written, visible, and actionable**.

Habakkuk 2:2 wasn't a suggestion—it was a strategy: *"Write the vision, and make it plain on tablets, that he may run who reads it."*

Here's what to do:

- **Write it** clearly—make it measurable and specific

127

- **Speak it** over your life daily—activate it with your words
- **Pray over it** consistently—birth it in the Spirit
- **Adjust it** as you grow—vision is alive, and it matures with you
- **Let it guide you**—use it to filter decisions, expenses, partnerships, and opportunities

A written vision becomes a **financial compass**. It helps you say yes to purpose and no to distractions. Your vision is not just a plan—it's a prophetic roadmap to your wealthy place.

Building a Kingdom-Sized Vision That Attracts Provision

Your financial vision must include **impact**—because Kingdom wealth is never just about personal comfort, it's about **divine assignment**.

Don't just think about your bills. Think about:

- **Nations to disciple**
- **Souls to reach**
- **Churches to plant and build**

- **Schools and hospitals to fund**
- **Young leaders to empower**
- **Families to deliver from generational poverty**

Psalm 2:8 says,

Ask of Me, and I will give You the nations for Your inheritance...

Psalm 2:8

You are called to think **beyond survival**, beyond status, beyond self. Let your financial vision be **Kingdom-sized**—because Heaven wants to finance more through you than just your lifestyle.

Dream on a **God scale**.

Vision attracts provision.

When your vision is aligned with God's heart, you will experience:

- **Uncommon favor**
- **Strategic relationships**
- **Divine ideas**
- **Supernatural acceleration**

Why? Because God provides for what He initiates.

Philippians 4:19 says,

My God shall supply all your need according to His riches in glory by Christ Jesus.

Philippians 4:19

But that verse doesn't apply to selfish ambition—it applies to **purpose-driven people** on Kingdom assignment.

Provision follows **vision**, not wishful thinking. If there is no clarity in your planning, there will be confusion in your provision.

Want to increase financially? Clarify your vision.

This is your moment to break free from:

- **Small thinking**
- **Aimless spending**
- **Financial wandering**
- **Visionless living**

God is calling you to **rise**, to **focus**, and to **build** with Him. Your vision is your permission to prosper. Your clarity is the seed of your capacity.

No more excuses. No more delays. No more "one day" thinking.

Today is the day to write the vision and run with it.

Your **wealthy place is waiting**. Let your vision lead you there.

Vision is not optional—it is essential. It disciplines your desires, directs your money, protects your focus, and qualifies you for provision.

A vague future produces vague finances. A clear vision prepares the way for divine increase.

Dream boldly. Plan clearly. Build prayerfully. Live intentionally.

CHAPTER 9

WEALTH AND SPIRITUAL WARFARE

CHAPTER NINE

WEALTH AND SPIRITUAL WARFARE

Recognizing the Spiritual Battle Behind Financial Resistance

Let's be clear: **money is not just economic—it is spiritual**. Behind every financial journey, there is a **warfare dimension**.

Wealth is not only a product of wisdom and work, but also the result of **spiritual victory** over invisible forces that resist increase.

Ephesians 6:12 says,

Wealth and Spiritual Warfare

We do not wrestle against flesh and blood, but against principalities, powers, rulers of darkness...

Ephesians 6:12

This includes:

- Forces that delay breakthrough
- Patterns that swallow profit
- Systems that cause sudden loss
- Curses that restrict expansion
- Temptations that corrupt the heart once wealth comes

As a believer, you cannot afford to be **financially blind and spiritually passive**.

The enemy knows that if you ever walk in true Kingdom wealth, you'll be dangerous to his agenda. So he fights—**strategically, persistently, and often invisibly**.

You've seen it before:

- People who work endlessly but never rise.
- Those who make money but lose it mysteriously.
- Business doors open, only to slam shut at the brink of success.

- Salary enters, but expenses erupt without explanation.
- Clients vanish. Deals collapse. Helpers disappear.

This is not always mismanagement. **Sometimes, it's war.** Spiritual warfare doesn't always show up with demons in dreams—it shows up as:

- **Repeated patterns of limitation**
- **Cycles of near-success failure**
- **Inexplicable delays**
- **Fear of prosperity**
- **Sudden setbacks after sowing or elevation**

When you start aligning with God's financial system, expect **resistance**. But also expect **victory**—if you know how to fight.

Financial warfare must be fought with **spiritual weapons**. You don't fight financial battles by complaining. You fight by:

- **Praying intentionally** over your finances
- **Fasting strategically** to break delays and expose hidden opposition

- **Renouncing generational curses** and demonic cycles
- **Speaking life** and favor over your work, bank accounts, contracts, and clients
- **Applying the blood of Jesus** to your finances
- **Sowing prophetically** to establish new cycles of breakthrough

Job 22:28 says,

You will also declare a thing, and it will be established for you...

Job 22:28

Silence is not neutrality—**silence is surrender**. You must rise in your authority and **declare war** on every spiritual force fighting your increase.

You are not a victim—you are a warrior. And your money is not carnal—it is **Kingdom ammunition**.

Breaking Mindsets and Reprogramming with Truth

Satan doesn't just attack your wallet—he **attacks your mind**.

If the enemy can:

- Convince you that wealth is evil
- Make you feel unworthy of abundance
- Keep you afraid of success
- Trap you in small thinking
- Weigh you down with guilt for desiring increase

…then he doesn't even need to touch your bank account. He just needs to corrupt your **belief system**.

Proverbs 23:7 says,

> *As a man thinks in his heart, so is he.*

Proverbs 23:7

If you think like a slave, you'll live like one—even with access to royalty. Poverty begins in the mind long before it manifests in your circumstances.

The enemy loves to plant lies like:

- "Money is not for spiritual people."
- "I'll never be rich unless I compromise."
- "Prosperity is only for the corrupt."
- "I don't need much; just enough to survive."

These thoughts don't sound evil—but they are **demonic limitations** dressed as humility. The only antidote to satanic financial programming is the **Word of God**.

Romans 12:2 says,

> *Be transformed by the renewing of your mind...*
>
> **Romans 12:2**

This means if you want to experience Kingdom wealth, you must **speak, study, and saturate** your mind with **financial truth from scripture**.

Here's how to begin:

1. **Study abundance scriptures** (e.g. Deuteronomy 8:18, Psalm 112, Proverbs 10:22, 3 John 1:2)
2. **Declare truth aloud** daily: "I am blessed to be a blessing." "I walk in abundance." "My hands are anointed to multiply wealth."
3. **Reject old thought patterns** and replace them with prophetic affirmations
4. **Meditate** until what you say becomes what you believe—and what you believe becomes what you walk in

You can't build wealth with a mind trained for survival. You must reprogram your heart for overflow. As your mind aligns with the Word, **the war shifts in your favor**.

Your **mouth is a weapon** in financial warfare.

Proverbs 18:21 says,

> *Death and life are in the power of the tongue...*
>
> **Proverbs 18:21**

That includes the life and death of your income, your business, your job, your ideas, and your opportunities.

Words to eliminate from your vocabulary:

- "I'm broke."
- "Money just disappears."
- "Nothing works for me."
- "We've never had anything in this family."
- "I'm not good with money."

These are not harmless phrases. They are **verbal agreements with limitation**.

Instead, speak the Word boldly:

- "Wealth and riches are in my house." (Psalm 112:3)
- "I have more than enough for every good work." (2 Cor. 9:8)
- "The Lord delights in my prosperity." (Psalm 35:27)
- "I lend to nations and do not borrow." (Deut. 28:12)

Your future responds to your confession. Use your tongue to prophesy your increase.

Activating Your Authority in Financial Realms

In spiritual warfare, you must **guard your gates**—especially the **eye gate** and the **ear gate**. What you watch and what you listen to shapes your mindset. And your mindset determines your financial atmosphere.

Romans 10:17 says,

So then faith comes by hearing, and hearing by the word of God.

Romans 10:17

But the reverse is also true: **fear comes by hearing**— especially when you constantly consume messages of scarcity, failure, and lack.

If all you listen to are complaints, bad news, and defeatist conversations, it won't be long before your spirit begins to reflect those sounds.

Feed your faith with:

- Teachings on biblical prosperity
- Kingdom success stories
- Testimonies of divine provision
- Scriptures that affirm your financial authority

Limit or eliminate content that glorifies poverty, mocks wealth, or ridicules faith-driven financial success. Faith must be **fed**—and your gates are the feeding grounds.

You are not called to **beg** the enemy—you are called to **command**.

Luke 10:19 says,

> *Behold, I give you authority… over all the power of the enemy...*
>
> **Luke 10:19**

You have legal and spiritual authority to:

- **Bind demonic forces** that restrict your increase

- **Break word curses** and financial delays
- **Loose angelic assistance** over your finances
- **Claim and protect your harvest**
- **Disarm satanic manipulation** in business, relationships, and investments

Stop praying timid prayers. Start issuing legal decrees in the spirit. Take your place as a **child, ambassador, and steward of God's Kingdom economy**. When you speak with revelation and authority, **heaven responds and hell retreats**.

In spiritual warfare, prophetic action is not superstition—it's **scriptural obedience**.

There's power in:

- **Anointing your hands** and declaring, "Whatever I touch prospers."
- **Laying hands on your wallet, business tools, phone, or computer** and speaking increase
- **Praying over your bank account and naming it 'overflow' or 'storehouse'**
- **Blessing your contracts, proposals, and projects with favor and fire**

Psalm 90:17 says,

> *Establish the work of our hands for us—yes, establish the work of our hands.*

Psalm 90:17

When you anoint and speak over your finances, you're not doing theatrics—you're **activating divine alignment**.

Use your oil. Use your words. Use your faith.

Activate your altar and command your wealth.

Enforcing Victory and Possessing Your Wealthy Place

Never forget this truth: **your finances are spiritual territory**. Every breakthrough you desire must be **fought for spiritually**, but it's not a battle you fight alone.

Colossians 2:15 reminds us that Jesus has *"disarmed principalities and powers..."*

The battle is real—but **the victory is already won** in Christ. Your job is not to strive—it is to **enforce victory**.

- Stand in your authority
- Speak what Heaven is saying
- Sow when God instructs
- Block every access point the enemy might use
- Keep your life clean, your mind renewed, and your gates guarded

You are not ordinary. Your destiny is not small. Your assignment is not natural. Therefore, your **financial life must be governed spiritually**.

This is not a season to be **casual**—it is a time to be **militant** in the Spirit.

- Stay alert—discern spiritual patterns and attacks
- Stay prayed up—build a strong altar around your finances
- Stay focused—don't be distracted by fear, greed, or comparison

The enemy doesn't play fair. But God doesn't lose battles.

1 John 5:4 says,

> *For everyone born of God overcomes the world...*

1 John 5:4

Decoding Divine Wealth

And Romans 8:37 declares,

In all these things, we are more than conquerors...

Romans 8:37

You are not just fighting for money—you are contending for **impact, inheritance, and Kingdom authority.**

Wealth requires war. But with God, you win—every time. It's time to rise like a warrior and take back what's yours.

- **Break every curse** that has limited your family for generations
- **Cancel every delay** that has held your harvest in limbo
- **Command your finances** to align with the Word
- **Declare abundance** over your household
- **Loose favor, contracts, and clients** to find you
- **Wage prophetic war** until the cycles shift permanently

Matthew 11:12 says,

The Kingdom of Heaven suffers violence, and the violent take it by force.

146

Wealth and Spiritual Warfare

Matthew 11:12

Now is the time to:

- Pray like never before
- Sow with precision
- Speak with fire
- Live in righteousness
- Take your seat in dominion

You are not begging for provision—you are taking possession.

- This is your time.
- This is your territory.
- This is your financial turning point.

Wealth is spiritual—and so is the warfare that surrounds it. To walk in true Kingdom prosperity, you must fight in prayer, renew your mind, guard your gates, and speak with authority.

Your money is not carnal. It is prophetic. It carries destiny. **Now rise, fight, and walk in your wealthy place.**

Decoding Divine Wealth

CHAPTER 10

SUSTAINING WEALTH THROUGH CHARACTER

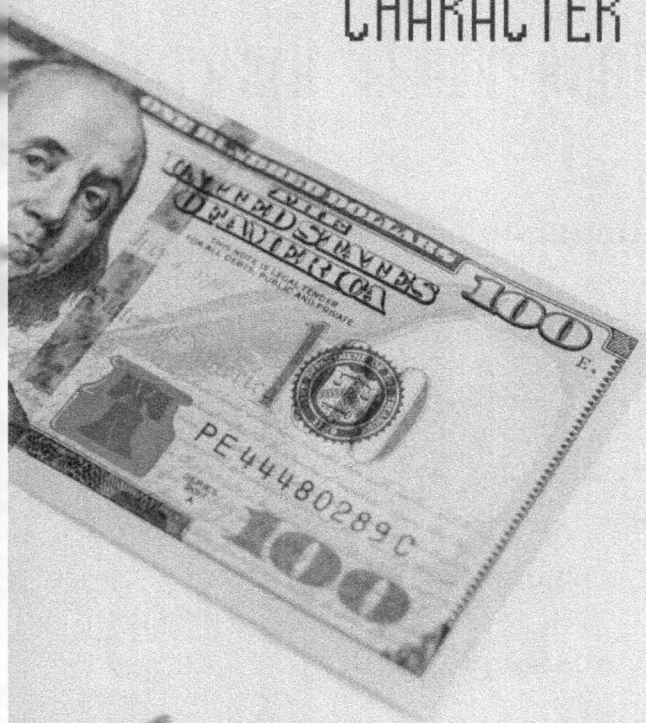

CHAPTER TEN

SUSTAINING WEALTH THROUGH CHARACTER

The Hidden Foundation of Enduring Wealth

Getting wealth is one level. **Sustaining it** is another.

Throughout history—and even today—we've seen individuals rise financially, only to **crash dramatically**. What caused the fall? Not lack of talent. Not lack of opportunity. But lack of **character**.

Character is the container of prosperity.

Without it, increase will collapse on itself.

Proverbs 11:3 says,

Sustaining Wealth through Character

The integrity of the upright will guide them, but the perversity of the unfaithful will destroy them.

Proverbs 11:3

- Without character, wealth becomes pride
- Without discipline, success breeds compromise
- Without integrity, doors open but don't last
- Without humility, promotion becomes poison

It is not just **anointing** or **intelligence** that keeps a man in his wealthy place. It is **godly character**.

Before God entrusts you with wealth, He will **test your heart**.

Why?

Because money has a way of **amplifying what's already inside**. If your character is shaky, wealth will expose it—and often destroy you.

- If money makes you arrogant, the problem isn't the money—it's your pride
- If success changes your attitude, it didn't change you—it revealed you
- If you mishandle little, much will not be a blessing—it will be your downfall

Luke 16:10 says,

He who is faithful in what is least is faithful also in much…

Luke 16:10

God watches how you:

- Treat others with small influence
- Handle resources no one sees
- Give when it's hard
- Speak when you have power
- Live when no one is watching

Character is your foundation. Wealth without it is a skyscraper on sand.

As your **net worth increases**, your **spiritual worth must increase faster**.

- **Integrity** ensures you stay trusted
- **Humility** keeps you grounded and grateful
- **Discipline** preserves your structure and boundaries
- **Generosity** protects your heart from greed and idolatry

God doesn't just want to bless you—He wants to **build you** into a man or woman who can carry His blessing **without breaking**.

1 Timothy 6:6 says,

> *Godliness with contentment is great gain.*
>
> **1 Timothy 6:6**

Many pursue wealth without watching their soul. But true Kingdom wealth requires that your **character rises with your income**—and even ahead of it.

Wealth in the wrong hands becomes a **weapon**. But in the hands of the righteous, it becomes a **blessing to generations**.

The Tests of Success—Temptation, Power, and Pride

One of the most overlooked truths about prosperity is this: **temptation increases with wealth**.

When you rise, you gain:

- **More attention**—from people with different motives

153

- **More options**—including ungodly ones
- **More influence**—which can be used for good or abused
- **More pressure**—to keep up appearances, protect status, or feed ego

Wealth expands your reach—but without character, it can also **expand your vulnerability**.

Proverbs 10:22 says,

The blessing of the Lord makes one rich, and He adds no sorrow with it.

Proverbs 10:22

But many add sorrow to themselves by chasing success **without spiritual accountability**.

If you don't kill pride before prosperity comes, it will **amplify and enslave you**. If you don't master lust, greed, and selfish ambition before increase arrives, wealth will feed the monsters within.

True success is not what you gain—it's what doesn't destroy you when you gain it.

Sustaining Wealth through Character

Wealth is a **magnifier**—not a transformer.

It doesn't change who you are. It simply **amplifies what already exists**.

- If you're selfish, money will magnify your selfishness
- If you're generous, money will expand your generosity
- If you're proud, money will turn that pride into arrogance
- If you're disciplined, money will help you build legacy

That's why you must build character **before** the increase comes. If not, the blessings you prayed for may become the very tools the enemy uses to derail you.

Ecclesiastes 7:14 says,

When times are good, be happy; but when times are bad, consider:
God has made the one as well as the other.

Ecclesiastes 7:14

Both success and struggle are **tests of character**.

Ask yourself now:

- Can God trust me with influence?
- Can God trust me with excess?

- Can I remain faithful, generous, and humble when doors open and overflow comes?

Wealth is not just a resource—it's a refiner. Prepare your character now.

Accountability, Motives, and the Safety of Submission

Gratitude is a safeguard for the wealthy. It keeps your heart humble and your eyes heavenward.

As God increases you, **never forget where you started**:

- Remember the nights you prayed with an empty wallet
- Remember the seasons you sowed in tears
- Remember when you had no platform, no resources, no connections

Deuteronomy 8:18 says,

But remember the Lord your God, for it is He who gives you power to get wealth...

Deuteronomy 8:18

God doesn't mind you rising, but He expects you to **remain rooted**.

Stay grateful:

- Don't let your status erase your story
- Don't let luxury silence your testimony
- Don't let abundance blind your worship

Every door, every deal, every dollar came by grace. The higher you go, the **lower your posture before God should be**.

Accountability is the shield of sustainable success.

No matter how anointed, gifted, or financially skilled you are—**you need voices that keep you anchored.**

- **Mentors** to correct you
- **Spiritual fathers or mothers** to guide you
- **Friends in purpose** to walk beside you
- **Advisers** to challenge your decisions

Proverbs 15:22 says,

Plans fail for lack of counsel, but with many advisers they succeed.

Proverbs 15:22

Success that isolates you is a setup for sabotage. Pride thrives in silence. Compromise hides in secrecy. But character is **shaped and sharpened in community**.

Surround yourself with those who won't be impressed by your wealth—but will be **committed to your well-being**.

Your **motive for wealth** determines how long it will last—and how useful it will be.

Ask yourself honestly:

- Do I want wealth to **impress others?**
- To **compete with others?**
- To **prove something to someone?**
- Or to **fulfill divine purpose?**

Proverbs 16:2 says,

All a person's ways seem pure to them, but motives are weighed by the Lord.

Proverbs 16:2

You can fool people with your presentation—but God sees your **intention**.

When your motive is:

- To fund the Kingdom
- To liberate your family
- To build solutions
- To raise others

…then your heart is in position for **lasting prosperity**.

God won't fund your ego. But He will fund your **assignment**.

Let's be clear: **character is not perfection—it is alignment.**

God isn't expecting flawless behavior. He's looking for:

- A **repentant heart** when you miss it
- A **teachable spirit** when corrected
- A **humble posture** in seasons of success
- A **submitted will** even when you could take control

Psalm 51:17 says,

> *The sacrifices of God are a broken spirit, a broken and contrite heart—these, O God, You will not despise.*
>
> **Psalm 51:17**

Wealth will test your:

159

- Ability to remain low when exalted
- Capacity to say "I was wrong" when corrected
- Discipline to choose righteousness when compromise is more profitable

Every new level of success comes with **new temptations**, and only those whose hearts stay aligned with God will **endure and flourish.**

Character doesn't mean you never fall—it means when you do, **you rise quickly, without pride, and keep your hands clean.**

Finishing Strong—Maturity, Repentance, and Endurance

In Kingdom prosperity, **finishing well is just as important as starting strong**.

History is full of men and women who:

- Rose with fire but ended in shame
- Built empires but lost their families
- Gained the world but forfeited their soul

Sustaining Wealth through Character

Proverbs 22:1 says,

> *A good name is to be chosen rather than great riches...*

Proverbs 22:1

- **Protect your name**—because your integrity is louder than your income
- **Protect your legacy**—because wealth is not just for now, it's for the next generation
- **Protect your soul**—because it's worth more than any bank account

The goal isn't just **accumulation**—it's **transference**. Not just success—but **significance**.

Wealth that corrupts you is not from God. But wealth that refines you, humbles you, and outlives you—that's Kingdom wealth.

Character is the highest form of wealth.

- A clean name is wealth
- A heart full of honor is wealth
- A reputation of faithfulness is wealth
- A legacy of obedience is wealth

Let people respect your money—but even more, let them **respect your walk with God**.

Psalm 112:6 says,

Surely the righteous will never be shaken; they will be remembered forever.

Psalm 112:6

Your house, cars, and investments are not your real legacy—your **character** is. Your **spiritual posture**, your **humility**, and your **impact** will echo into eternity.

Let your name be one that **opens doors, heals wounds, and inspires generations**. Pray not just for more money—but for **more maturity**.

Ask God:

- "Make me a vessel You can trust."
- "Refine my character before You increase my platform."
- "Let my roots go deep, even as my influence grows wide."
- "Help me never exalt the blessing above the Blesser."

Psalm 1:3 says,

He shall be like a tree planted by rivers of water... and whatever he does shall prosper.

Psalm 1:3

You were not just born to be rich—you were born to be **righteous and rooted**. God doesn't want to just raise wealthy people—He wants to raise **wise, grounded, Kingdom stewards**.

Let God **build you** even as He **blesses you**. Sustaining wealth is not just about financial literacy—it's about **spiritual maturity**.

Without character, blessings collapse. But with integrity, humility, and submission, your wealth becomes a tool for **legacy and eternal impact**.

Rise. Grow. Mature. Finish well.

Decoding Divine Wealth

CHAPTER 11

KINGDOM WEALTH AND DIVINE ASSIGNMENT

CHAPTER ELEVEN

KINGDOM WEALTH AND DIVINE ASSIGNMENT

Wealth as a Tool for Purpose, Not a Replacement for It

You were not sent to earth simply to **make a living**—you were sent to **fulfil a divine assignment**. Wealth, in the Kingdom, is never an end in itself—it is a **tool to fulfil calling**.

- Money is a servant, not a master
- Increase is a resource, not your identity
- Prosperity is a platform for purpose, not a replacement for it

Kingdom Wealth and Divine Assignment

When you forget your assignment, you'll misuse your abundance. But when your wealth is aligned with divine calling, it becomes a **weapon of transformation**.

2 Corinthians 9:8 says,

God is able to bless you abundantly… so that in all things at all times… you will abound in every good work.

2 Corinthians 9:8

That "good work" is your **assignment**. And your wealth is meant to support it.

In God's economy, **provision follows purpose**.

- God doesn't just bless ideas—He blesses **assignments**
- He funds what He authors
- He releases resources where there is a **divine mandate**

Your calling determines the scale of your financial need. And when you pursue that calling with obedience, the resources will **flow to meet the mission**.

Chase money, and you may end up frustrated. But **chase purpose**, and money will pursue you.

Matthew 6:33 echoes this truth:

Seek first the Kingdom of God and His righteousness, and all these things shall be added to you.

Matthew 6:33

You were not designed to run after things. You were created to run after God's will—and let things **find you in alignment**.

Pause and reflect:

What has God called you to build, fund, or advance?

- A ministry?
- A business with Kingdom values?
- A school? A center for transformation?
- A media platform to spread truth?
- A revival movement in your city or region?

Once you answer that question, every income stream should begin to **align with that assignment**.

When wealth is disconnected from purpose, it becomes **wasteful**—even dangerous. But when wealth flows in sync with your divine calling, it becomes **worship**.

168

Kingdom Wealth and Divine Assignment

Psalm 90:17 says,

Let the favor of the Lord our God be upon us, and establish the work of our hands for us...

Psalm 90:17

Let God **establish your hands**, so your wealth becomes a **living altar of obedience.**

Let Your Treasure Follow Your Calling

Purpose gives wealth direction.

Without a clear sense of assignment:

- You'll start comparing your income with someone else's
- You'll try to replicate someone else's business, not realizing your grace is different
- You'll chase what's trending, rather than what's anointed
- You'll feel busy—but remain unfulfilled

But when you know your divine assignment:

- You focus on what matters
- You steward your wealth intentionally

169

- You stop competing—and start completing your part in God's bigger picture
- You measure success by **obedience**, not by applause

Galatians 6:4 says,

Each one should test their own actions. Then they can take pride in themselves alone, without comparing themselves to someone else.

Galatians 6:4

Your financial path is **assignment-specific**. Run your race. Fund your lane. Finish your course. A true Kingdom steward lets their **budget reflect their burden**.

If your heart burns for:

- **Souls** — invest in missions and evangelism
- **Youth** — fund mentorship programs, education, or outreach
- **Media** — support Kingdom content creators and digital platforms
- **Health** — sponsor clinics, healing meetings, and wellness outreach
- **The Church** — build and equip ministries and ministers

Kingdom Wealth and Divine Assignment

Luke 12:34 says,

For where your treasure is, there your heart will be also.

Luke 12:34

But the reverse is equally powerful: **where your heart is, your treasure should follow.** Don't just say you care—**sow into what you care about.** Let your giving preach louder than your words.

This is how wealth becomes **an extension of your calling**, not a distraction from it.

You are not called to **fund everything**—but you are called to **fund what aligns with your divine mandate**.

- You don't need to say "yes" to every good cause
- You need to say "yes" to the causes tied to your calling
- Purpose **protects you from financial confusion and pressure**

2 Corinthians 10:13 says,

We will not boast beyond measure, but within the limits of the sphere which God appointed us...

2 Corinthians 10:13

When you try to fund what isn't your assignment:

- You wear yourself out
- You sow without grace
- You miss the joy of obedience

But when you **focus your financial flow**, your impact multiplies. Purpose brings precision. And **precision brings power.**

Finding Fulfillment Through Purpose-Aligned Prosperity

God's desire is for you to enjoy His blessings, but **prosperity is not the final destination—it is a divine tool for Kingdom expansion.**

Yes, you can have a beautiful house.

Yes, you can drive a great car.

Yes, you can enjoy comfort and overflow.

But **those are not the mission**. They are the **overflow**, not the **objective**.

The real goal is:

- To fund the preaching of the gospel
- To build and support local churches
- To disciple nations through education, business, media, and government
- To leave a legacy that reflects God, not just wealth

Zechariah 1:17 says,

> *My cities shall again spread out through prosperity; the Lord will again comfort Zion, and will again choose Jerusalem.*

Zechariah 1:17

Prosperity is meant to **mobilize revival**, not just **material reward**.

Don't let the reward become your reason. Let the **Kingdom remain your compass.**

There is a kind of joy that money alone can't produce. It's the joy of knowing that you are:

- **Changing lives**
- **Funding transformation**
- **Walking in divine obedience**
- **Building something eternal**

Ecclesiastes 2:26 says,

Decoding Divine Wealth

To the person who pleases Him, God gives wisdom, knowledge and happiness...

Ecclesiastes 2:26

Purpose-aligned prosperity brings:

- **Peace, not pressure**
- **Fulfilment, not just finances**
- **Joy, not just luxury**

You can have millions and still feel empty. But when every dollar flows from divine purpose, **you sleep with fulfillment and rise with fire**.

Purpose makes wealth worth it. **Comparison is the enemy of contentment.** And envy is the thief of clarity.

Stay in your lane. You are not called to copy—you're called to **conquer your specific territory**.

- Don't mimic someone else's success
- Don't chase trends that don't fit your grace
- Don't build what God never assigned to you

Romans 12:6 reminds us,

Kingdom Wealth and Divine Assignment

Having then gifts differing according to the grace that is given to us, let us use them…

Romans 12:6

There is:

- **Grace for your assignment**
- **Provision for your obedience**
- **Prosperity for your specific calling**

You don't need to do what they do. Just do what **God sent you to do**—and do it faithfully.

Living for Eternal Reward and Finishing Your Financial Race Well

Your **wealth should preach.**

It should tell a story—not just of success, but of **redemption, wisdom,** and **obedience.** Let your house, your giving, your business, and your generosity all declare: **"This is what the Lord has done."**

Psalm 126:3 says,

The Lord has done great things for us, and we are glad.

Psalm 126:3

Every financial increase should:

- Reflect the **faithfulness of God**
- Echo the **wisdom of divine alignment**
- Advance the **gospel of Jesus Christ**
- Inspire others to pursue purpose, not just possessions

Let your life be a **living message**—a testimony that wealth, when submitted to purpose, becomes a tool for eternal impact.

Everything you have should point in one direction—**divine assignment**.

- Let every income stream support your vision
- Let every investment reflect your values
- Let every opportunity take you deeper into God's purpose

If something pulls you **away** from your calling—**no matter how profitable it is**, it's not worth the cost.

Mark 8:36 says,

What shall it profit a man, if he gains the whole world, and loses his soul?

Mark 8:36

You were not created for random success—you were created for **strategic significance**. And **purpose-aligned prosperity** is the only kind that endures.

There will come a day when you'll stand before the One who gave you the gift of life—and wealth.

And on that day, God will not ask:

- How much did you make?
- How many houses did you buy?
- How far did your brand go?

He will ask:

- **What did you do with what I gave you?**
- **Whom did you serve?**
- **What did your wealth fund?**
- **How did you use your influence for My Kingdom?**

2 Corinthians 5:10 reminds us,

> *For we must all appear before the judgment seat of Christ...*

2 Corinthians 5:10

So live with the end in mind. Build with eternity in view. Let every coin, contract, client, and career move reflect your desire to **hear Him say, "Well done."**

Your wealth is not random—it is **assignment-specific.** It must align with your divine purpose, reflect your Kingdom values, and speak of your eternal hope.

Live on assignment. Prosper on purpose. Finish with honour.

CHAPTER 12

FINANCIAL WHOLENESS AND INNER HEALING

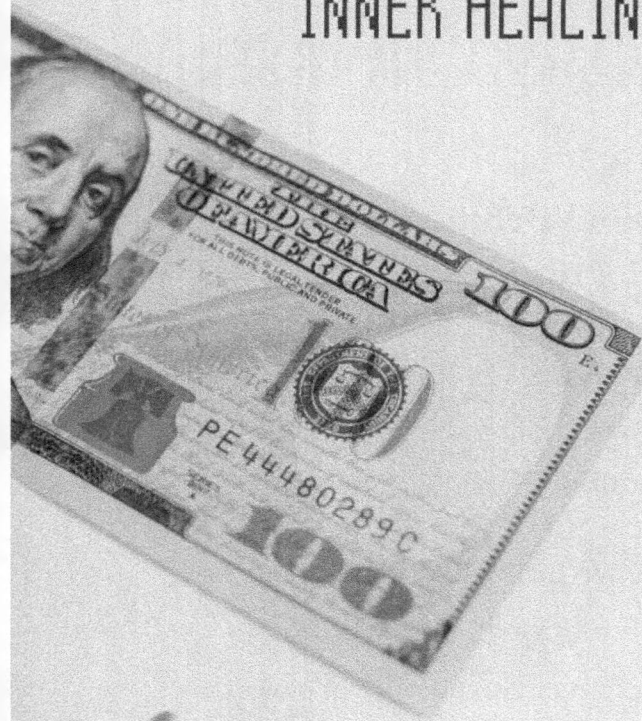

CHAPTER TWELVE

FINANCIAL WHOLENESS AND INNER HEALING

Healing the Soul Behind the Pursuit of Prosperity

You cannot walk in sustained, God-ordained prosperity with a **fractured soul**. Many people are chasing wealth not from vision—but from **wounds**.

- Trying to earn love through financial success
- Seeking validation through possessions
- Using money to cover shame or prove worth
- Hoping that success will silence inner rejection

But here's the truth: **money doesn't heal—God does.**

Financial Wholeness and Inner Healing

3 John 1:2 says,

Beloved, I pray that you may prosper in all things and be in health, just as your soul prospers.

3 John 1:2

If your soul is broken, prosperity becomes dangerous. But when your soul is healed, money becomes **a tool, not a drug**.

You don't need more money to feel whole—you need more of God's love and truth to heal what's been broken. Before you pursue wealth, ask yourself:

"Why do I want to prosper?"

Is it...

- Fear of poverty?
- A desire to prove others wrong?
- Childhood trauma or rejection?
- Pressure from culture or family?
- A need to feel important?

These motives may be common—but they are not safe. When wealth flows from **wounded ambition**, it becomes polluted—no matter how impressive it looks externally.

Decoding Divine Wealth

James 4:3 warns,

You ask and do not receive, because you ask amiss, that you may spend it on your pleasures.

James 4:3

If your desire for wealth is driven by pain, you will chase it endlessly—yet never feel satisfied. But when God heals the root, He purifies the pursuit. And you begin to **build from wholeness, not brokenness**.

Wholeness attracts favor.

- Desperation clouds judgment.
- Brokenness creates confusion.

But healing births clarity.

When your heart is whole:

- You make better business and investment decisions
- You attract partners who respect your peace—not manipulate your pain
- You're not driven by "proving a point," but by fulfilling a purpose

- You no longer self-sabotage when opportunities come
- You walk with a quiet confidence that magnetizes favor

Proverbs 4:23 says,

Above all else, guard your heart, for everything you do flows from it.

Proverbs 4:23

Want to prosper deeply and lastingly? Let God **heal your heart**, and you will begin to prosper without fear, pressure, or pretence.

Letting God Father Your Heart and Purify Your Motives

There are people who **unconsciously sabotage financial increase**—not because they are lazy or unskilled, but because deep down, **they don't believe they're worthy**.

They may:

- Decline life-changing opportunities
- Undervalue their services or gifts
- Mishandle wealth the moment it arrives

183

- Get uncomfortable with abundance
- Push away divine connections out of fear or shame

Why? Because **inner brokenness is louder than external blessings.**

Isaiah 61:1 says,

He has sent Me to heal the brokenhearted, to proclaim liberty to the captives…

Isaiah 61:1

And that includes captives of **financial limitation rooted in emotional pain.**

Until your identity is healed, you will subconsciously reject the very harvests you're praying for. Healing is not optional—it is **essential** for sustainable Kingdom wealth.

Before you try to master your finances, allow God to **father your heart.**

Let Him:

- **Affirm your identity** as His beloved
- **Heal the wounds** of past rejection, neglect, or abuse
- **Break the fear** of failure or not being enough

184

- **Lift the shame** that's hidden behind your ambition

Romans 8:15 says,

You did not receive a spirit of bondage again to fear, but you received the Spirit of adoption, by whom we cry, 'Abba, Father.'

Romans 8:15

When you receive healing from the Father:

- You stop performing for approval
- You stop overworking to feel worthy
- You start stewarding wealth from a place of rest and joy
- You give and receive with freedom—not fear

Inner healing is financial healing. When your soul prospers, every area of your life begins to reflect the freedom of the Kingdom.

Money is not medication.

Don't use it to:

- Numb emotional pain
- Silence the ache of rejection
- Cover broken relationships

185

- Escape loneliness or emptiness

God wants to go deep—because He's planning to **bless you wide**.

Psalm 147:3 says,

He heals the brokenhearted and binds up their wounds.

Psalm 147:3

Let Him touch the parts of you that success can't reach. Let Him clean the places that applause can't heal. When God **heals the inner man,** the outer man begins to prosper with peace, stability, and spiritual authority.

You don't need to impress anyone. You just need to be whole.

Releasing Offense, Bitterness, and Emotional Blockages

Bitterness is **a spiritual tax** you cannot afford to pay. Unforgiveness may feel justified, but it is **spiritually expensive**. It:

- Blocks your flow of revelation

- Interrupts divine instruction
- Clouds your discernment
- Delays answered prayer
- Distorts how you handle relationships and resources

Mark 11:25 says,

And when you stand praying, if you hold anything against anyone, forgive them, so that your Father in heaven may forgive you...

Mark 11:25

Forgiveness is not weakness—it is warfare.

When you let people go, you're not excusing the offense— you're severing the spiritual leash that ties your destiny to pain.

You cannot enter your **wealthy place** while dragging **baggage of bitterness** behind you. Release them—and you'll release yourself.

Offense is one of the enemy's most subtle weapons against destiny.

It:

- Drains your joy

- Distracts your focus
- Makes you reactive instead of strategic
- Corrupts your discernment
- Slows your spiritual and financial momentum

Proverbs 18:19 says,

> *A brother offended is harder to win than a strong city...*
>
> **Proverbs 18:19**

Offense doesn't just block relationships—it **builds emotional prisons**. And when your heart is heavy, your hands can't build.

You start making financial decisions out of pain instead of purpose. You begin to isolate from wise counsel. You sow less, serve less, dream less.

Let it go. Your freedom is more valuable than your grudge.

Wholeness begins with **honesty.**

Ask the Holy Spirit:

- "What's still bleeding inside me?"
- "What pain am I hiding behind my ambition?"

- "What disappointments have hardened my faith?"
- "Who am I still angry with in secret?"

Psalm 139:23–24 says,

Search me, O God, and know my heart; test me and know my anxious thoughts...

Psalm 139:23-24

The Spirit of God is both the **Surgeon** and the **Healer**. He doesn't expose to embarrass—He exposes to restore.

Let Him clean what you've ignored. Let Him comfort what you've covered. Let Him restore what pain tried to define. Because your next level of wealth will require a deeper level of **wholeness.**

Embracing the Process of Wholeness and Identity Restoration

God doesn't just want to bless your hands—He wants to **heal your heart**.

Don't chase after increase while bleeding internally. Don't pursue overflow while neglecting the **invisible fractures** in your soul.

189

Yes, He is Jehovah Jireh—your Provider. But He is also Jehovah Rapha—your **Healer**.

Isaiah 53:5 reminds us, *"By His wounds we are healed."* That includes healing from:

- Rejection
- Comparison
- Insecurity
- Parental wounds
- Church wounds
- Betrayal and disappointment

Let Him do both. Let Him **bless and rebuild**. Let Him increase and restore. Wholeness is wealth. Healing is holy. And freedom is your inheritance.

Healing is a process—and it's worth every moment.

Don't rush past your pain.

- Sit with God.
- Journal your journey.
- Weep if necessary.
- Rest when needed.

But whatever you do—**don't numb it or suppress it**.

Psalm 34:18 says,

> *The Lord is close to the brokenhearted and saves those who are crushed in spirit.*

Psalm 34:18

God can turn your deepest wound into your greatest **wealth of wisdom**.

- He can turn your pain into power.
- He can use your scars as signposts for others.

Healing doesn't make you weak—it makes you **whole, wise, and wealthy in ways money cannot buy**.

Let these words sink into your spirit:

- **You are loved.**
- **You are chosen.**
- **You are not late.**
- **You are not disqualified.**
- **You are not too broken to be blessed.**

God never gives up mid-process.

Philippians 1:6 says,

191

Decoding Divine Wealth

He who began a good work in you will carry it on to completion...

Philippians 1:6

- Let Him finish the work.
- Let Him rebuild your identity.
- Let Him rewire your beliefs.
- Let Him renew your joy.

Because when your soul is whole, your wealth will have depth. And your prosperity will not just touch your hands—but also reflect His healing glory through your life.

True Kingdom prosperity flows from **a healed, whole, and surrendered heart**. Until the inner man is well, the outer man cannot carry lasting increase.

Let God heal you deeply so He can trust you fully. And let your financial journey begin from **peace, identity, and divine freedom.**

CHAPTER 13

THE COVENANT OF KINGDOM PROSPERITY

CHAPTER THIRTEEN

THE COVENANT OF KINGDOM PROSPERITY

Wealth Rooted in Covenant, Not Competition

God is not moved by hustle—He is moved by **covenant**.

In the Kingdom, prosperity is not earned by striving, nor sustained by competition. It is accessed and preserved through your **covenant relationship with God**.

Deuteronomy 8:18 says,

But you shall remember the Lord your God, for it is He who gives you power to get wealth, that He may establish His covenant…

Deuteronomy 8:18

The Covenant of Kingdom Prosperity

- Covenant, not competition, is your advantage.
- Covenant, not culture, defines your economic outlook.
- Covenant, not capitalism, is your foundation for financial security.

The world builds wealth on pressure and performance. But the Kingdom builds on **promise and partnership** with God.

Until you understand covenant, you'll keep striving for what grace has already made available. A **covenant** is not a casual agreement—it is a **sacred bond sealed by divine authority**.

God made a covenant with Abraham. That covenant included:

- Blessing
- Multiplication
- Land
- Influence
- Generational wealth

Galatians 3:29 reveals something powerful: *"If you are Christ's, then you are Abraham's seed, and heirs according to the promise."*

That means if you are born again:

- You are not chasing wealth—you're **inheriting it by covenant**
- You are not hoping to be blessed—you're already **positioned in promise**
- You don't have to beg for provision—it is your **legal birthright**

Covenant is not just spiritual—it has **economic dimensions**. You must learn to walk in it intentionally. You are not a beggar in God's economy—you are a **son in covenant**.

Romans 8:17 says,

> *If children, then heirs—heirs of God and joint heirs with Christ...*
>
> **Romans 8:17**

When you forget your covenant:

- You pray like a slave, not a son

196

- You work like an orphan, not a steward
- You panic when bills come, rather than command your provision

But when you remember your covenant:

- You speak with authority
- You tithe with joy
- You give with boldness
- You expect miracles, not as a favor, but as a **family right**

Stop hustling to be blessed—**stand in your covenant** and walk like the heir that you are.

Obedience—The Bridge Between Promise and Possession

Every covenant comes with **terms**—and in the Kingdom, the blessing of the covenant is activated by **obedience**.

God will always honor His part. But He expects you to:

- Walk in righteousness
- Honor His Word
- Obey divine instructions

- Steward what He gives
- Trust Him even when it doesn't make sense

Deuteronomy 28:1–2 says,

If you fully obey the Lord your God... all these blessings will come upon you and overtake you...

Deuteronomy 28:1-2

Obedience is not a burden—it is a **bridge**.

- A bridge from promise to possession
- A bridge from prophecy to manifestation
- A bridge from "I believe" to "I receive"

You don't earn your blessing, but **you unlock its manifestation** through surrendered, joyful obedience. Every divine instruction is a **setup for supernatural provision**.

Your:

- **Tithe** is not a tax—it's a covenant act of honor
- **Offerings** are not charity—they're seeds into divine purpose

- **Sacrifices** are not loss—they are keys that open portals of increase
- **Prompt obedience** to Spirit-led instructions often precedes explosive breakthroughs

Psalm 50:5 says,

Gather My saints together to Me, those who have made a covenant with Me by sacrifice.

Psalm 50:5

In the Kingdom, wealth flows **through the gate of obedience**. And every act of covenant obedience triggers a **response from Heaven**.

Your giving isn't just generosity—it's **spiritual alignment**.

Covenant is not just something you believe—it's something you **live conscious of daily**.

- **Declare it** over your life: "I am the seed of Abraham. I walk in divine wealth."
- **Speak it** over your finances: "Provision is my covenant right."
- **Remember it** in moments of fear: "God is my source—not man, not systems."

- **Respond to it** with joy and trust: "I obey because I'm in covenant, not to get in covenant."

When you live covenant-conscious:

- Fear dies
- Begging stops
- Panic ends
- Faith rises
- Joy increases

Psalm 89:34 says,

My covenant I will not break, nor alter the word that has gone out of My lips.

Psalm 89:34

If God can't break His covenant, neither can the economy, inflation, or adversity break your **access to divine provision**.

Supernatural Confidence in a Natural Crisis

Covenant gives you **unshakable confidence**—not in circumstances, but in **your source**.

The Covenant of Kingdom Prosperity

Psalm 37:19 says,

> *In the days of famine they shall be satisfied.*

Psalm 37:19

When you're covenant-minded:

- Famine doesn't frighten you
- Economic downturns don't dictate your decisions
- Business slowdowns don't destabilize your peace
- Delays don't disqualify your destiny

Why? Because your provision is not sourced from:

- A salary
- A government system
- A trending industry
- A currency that fluctuates

Your source is **Jehovah Jireh**—the God who doesn't run out. When others fear recession, covenant people prepare for elevation.

You may live **in the world,** but you operate by the **laws of a higher Kingdom.**

John 17:16 says,

They are not of the world, even as I am not of it.

John 17:16

You're not governed by:

- Inflation
- Market crashes
- Political instability
- Scarcity-driven headlines

You are governed by:

- **Divine principles**
- **Covenant promises**
- **Supernatural supply lines**
- **Spiritual wisdom that overrides worldly fear**

Your Father is not limited. And because you're a **Kingdom citizen**, your lifestyle must reflect His **stability and abundance**, even in unstable times.

Covenant living lifts you **above the chaos** and teaches you to thrive when others are merely trying to survive.

Your **words must match your covenant.**

Proverbs 18:21 says,

> *Death and life are in the power of the tongue…*

Proverbs 18:21

If your mouth speaks fear while your heart holds faith—you **cancel your own authority**.

- Don't say "The economy is hard"—say "God supplies all my needs."
- Don't say "Money is tight"—say "I walk in overflow."
- Don't say "Nothing is working"—say "The Lord delights in my prosperity."
- Don't say "I don't know what to do"—say "I have divine strategies and wisdom."

Your covenant is **voice-activated**. Speak what Heaven has said. Let your mouth become the **echo of your covenant confidence**.

Walking Boldly in Your Covenant Identity

You are not ordinary—you are a **covenant carrier**.

That means:

- You are **marked by God**

- You are **backed by Heaven**
- You are **covered in times of adversity**
- You are **empowered to prosper on purpose**

Isaiah 60:1–2 says,

Arise, shine; for your light has come! And the glory of the Lord is risen upon you... the Lord will arise over you, and His glory will be seen upon you.

Isaiah 60:1-2

Even in gross darkness, **the covenant will make you shine.**

You are not hustling like the world. You are not scrambling for survival. You are not desperate or forsaken. You are a **son of the covenant**, and your life must reflect it.

Stand in your covenant rights.

Don't just hope for provision—**claim it as your inheritance.** Don't just pray timid prayers—**pray as a rightful heir.**

Romans 8:17 reminds us: *"If children, then heirs..."*

That means:

- You have legal access
- You have supernatural covering
- You have generational responsibility
- You have divine confidence

God hasn't forgotten you. He's simply waiting for you to remember: **Who you are. What you carry. And what you're entitled to.**

This is your **covenant season**.

- **Wake up to it**—don't live beneath your privileges
- **Walk in it**—live with intentionality and Kingdom mindset
- **War for it**—fight the lies, doubt, fear, and limitations
- **Prosper in it**—with confidence, generosity, and peace

Galatians 3:14 says,

That the blessing of Abraham might come upon the Gentiles in Christ Jesus...

Galatians 3:14

That blessing is:

- Multigenerational

- Multidimensional
- Supernatural
- Irrevocable

The blessing of Abraham is on you. **Now act like it. Live like it. Speak like it. Prosper like it.**

Kingdom prosperity is not a lucky break—it is your **covenant inheritance.**

You are not striving to get blessed—you are simply learning to **stand in what's already yours** through Christ. Walk boldly. Sow fearlessly. Declare confidently. Obey joyfully.

You are a covenant person—and it's time your life reflects it.

CHAPTER 14

POSITIONED FOR OVERFLOW

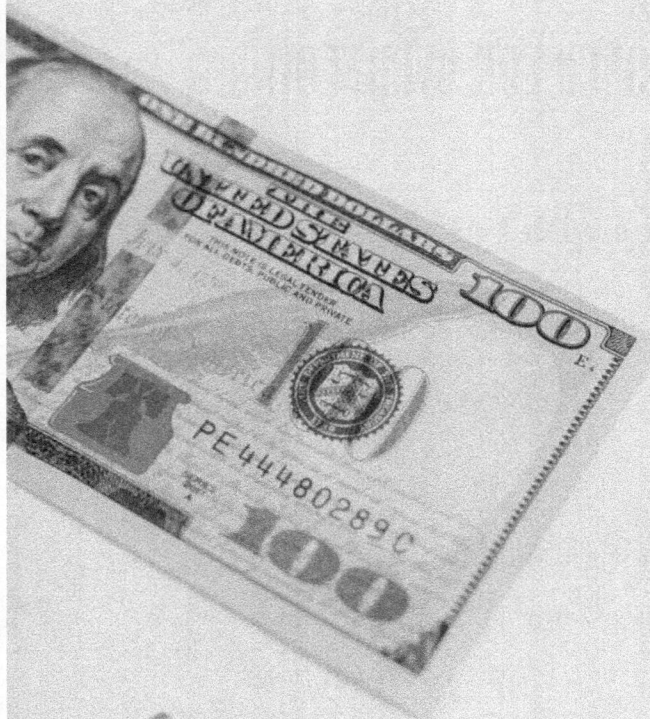

CHAPTER FOURTEEN

POSITIONED FOR OVERFLOW

Overflow Begins with Posture, Not Pressure

You were not created to just scrape by—**overflow is your portion**.

In the Kingdom:

- "Enough" is not the final destination
- "Barely surviving" is not your inheritance
- "More than enough" is the covenant norm

Psalm 23:5 says,

> *You anoint my head with oil; my cup runs over.*

Psalm 23:5

But overflow is not just about effort—it's about **posture**.

God responds to:

- **Surrendered hearts**
- **Obedient hands**
- **Open vessels**
- **Faith-filled declarations**

You don't qualify for overflow by stress. You receive it by **alignment**. Overflow begins with how you think, how you speak, how you obey, and how you position your life for divine release.

Your posture determines your portion.

- If you think small, you'll live small
- If you speak lack, you'll attract limitation
- If you expect barely enough, you'll rarely see more than that

Isaiah 54:2 says,

> *Enlarge the place of your tent... stretch out... do not hold back.*

Isaiah 54:2

God is willing—but are you **positioned to receive?**

To walk in overflow, you must:

- **Expand your faith**—dream on a God-sized scale
- **Speak abundance**—align your language with Heaven
- **Plan with vision**—create structure for increase
- **Sow in expectation**—give as though harvest is inevitable

Your mind must stretch before your money grows. Your vision must deepen before your vault expands.

Overflow is not an accident. It is the result of **intentional positioning. Overflow is never for ego—it is always for Kingdom stewardship.**

When God gives you more than enough, it's not so you can:

- Flaunt it
- Hoard it
- Worship it
- Compete with others

It's so you can:

- **Fund Kingdom projects**
- **Rescue the hurting**
- **Establish righteousness in the earth**
- **Multiply impact across generations**

2 Corinthians 9:11 says,

You will be enriched in every way so that you can be generous on every occasion...

2 Corinthians 9:11

You are not the **final destination** of the overflow—you are the **distribution channel**. And the more God can trust you with, the more He will release through you.

Prepare Your Structure to Carry Supernatural Supply

Overflow is not random—it is responsive.

God doesn't waste resources. He pours into **prepared vessels**.

2 Kings 4 tells the story of a widow whose oil kept flowing **as long as there were vessels**.

When the vessels stopped, the flow stopped.

That principle still applies:

- **No systems—no surplus**
- **No vision—no volume**
- **No containers—no continuous flow**

Overflow requires:

- **Financial structure**—budgets, accounts, investments
- **Business structure**—teams, offers, follow-up systems
- **Mental structure**—clear goals and focus
- **Spiritual structure**—disciplined giving, prayer, and stewardship

Proverbs 24:3–4 says,

By wisdom a house is built, and through understanding it is established; through knowledge its rooms are filled with rare and beautiful treasures.

Proverbs 24:3-4

God will not fill what you won't build. So if you're asking for overflow—**prepare for it.**

Sowing is the gateway to overflow.

2 Corinthians 9:10 says,

Now may He who supplies seed to the sower... supply and multiply the seed you have sown...

2 Corinthians 9:10

God doesn't give seed to the stingy—He gives it to the **sower.**

If you want to walk in consistent overflow:

- Become **generous by nature**
- Become **predictable in giving**
- Become **prompt in obedience**
- Become **joyful in sacrifice**

Hoarding shuts down Heaven. But generosity turns on a faucet that **never runs dry**.

Luke 6:38 says,

Give, and it shall be given to you...

Luke 6:38

Not "pray," not "worry," not "complain"—**give.**

213

Overflow is not unlocked through emotion. It's unlocked through **action rooted in covenant**.

Overflow begins with expectation.

Mark 11:24 says,

Whatever things you ask when you pray, believe that you receive them, and you will have them.

Mark 11:24

Faith creates the atmosphere where abundance manifests.

You must:

- **Expect provision**—not as a possibility, but as a certainty
- **Speak it boldly**—"My cup runs over. Doors are opening. I am a distributor of divine wealth."
- **Walk like it's coming**—prepare before the harvest
- **Live like God is faithful**—not wavering when things look slow

Doubt delays. Fear frustrates. But faith activates.

Expectancy is the breeding ground for overflow.

If your mouth and your mindset are ready—**your manifestation won't be far behind.**

Stewarding the Flow—Wisdom, Discipline, and Worship

Overflow is not just about sudden breakthrough—it's about sustained cycles of increase. God doesn't bless randomly. He blesses according to **divine rhythms**.

Genesis 8:22 says,

As long as the earth remains, seedtime and harvest… shall not cease.

Genesis 8:22

That means:

- There are **seasons of sowing** and **seasons of reaping**
- There are **windows of opportunity** that require obedience
- There are **cycles of generosity** that create cycles of overflow

You don't need a miracle every month—you need **mastery of divine cycles.**

When you:

- Stay consistent in giving
- Honor seasons of sacrifice
- Maintain discipline during abundance
- Obey the Spirit's timing

...you begin to walk in **sustained provision**, not just emergency interventions.

Overflow isn't an event—it's a **way of life**.

Overflow demands wisdom.

Many people pray for abundance—then mismanage it when it comes. God is not just looking for receivers—He's looking for **wise stewards**.

Proverbs 21:20 says,

The wise store up choice food and olive oil, but fools gulp theirs down.

Proverbs 21:20

When overflow comes:

- Don't blow it—**budget it**
- Don't flaunt it—**invest it**

- Don't hoard it—**sow it strategically**
- Don't forget God—**worship with it**

Overflow is not a license to be reckless—it's a test of maturity. If you're faithful with much, more will come. But if you waste it, the cycle may close.

Overflow is **multi-generational wealth in seed form**—handle it with the future in mind.

Overflow should never become your idol—it should always increase your intimacy with God.

Deuteronomy 8:10 says,

When you have eaten and are satisfied, praise the Lord your God…
Deuteronomy 8:10

When God increases you:

- Let your **worship grow** with your wealth
- Let your **gratitude deepen** with every harvest
- Let your **generosity expand** as doors open
- Let your **awe remain childlike**, no matter how high you rise

Overflow is not just financial—it's **spiritual confirmation** that Heaven can trust you. Don't let increase make you arrogant. Let it make you more **aware of the One who gave it.**

The more He gives you, the more you should say: "Lord, it's all Yours. Use me."

Overflow Is Your Covenant Normal, not a Rare Event

- You were not created for scarcity.
- You were not born to struggle.
- You were designed by God to live in **overflow.**

Deuteronomy 28:12 declares,

> *You shall lend to many nations, but you shall not borrow.*
>
> **Deuteronomy 28:12**

That's not just a dream—that's your **Kingdom birthright.**

You were born to:

- Lend, not borrow
- Fund vision, not chase survival

218

- Empower others, not beg for scraps
- Leave inheritance, not debt
- Build systems, not survive in cycles

God's plan has always been **abundance with assignment**—not luxury without purpose. Let this truth anchor your expectations:

Overflow is your default—not your exception.

Stop waiting for overflow as if it's a once-in-a-lifetime moment. **Start declaring it as your daily reality.**

- Speak it: "I walk in divine abundance."
- Expect it: "Favor surrounds me like a shield."
- Prepare for it: "My systems are ready for supernatural supply."
- Walk in it: "I am a distributor of Kingdom wealth."

John 10:10 (AMP) says,

*I came that they may have and enjoy life, and have it in abundance—
to the full, till it overflows.*

John 10:10 (AMP)

That's not just spiritual—it's financial. Relational. Emotional. Kingdom-wide.

Overflow is not just what you receive—it's what you release. And it's time for you to stop chasing it—and **start living in it.**

You are not a victim of economic cycles. You are not at the mercy of market trends. You are **in covenant. Under blessing. Positioned for overflow.**

Psalm 1:3 says,

> *Whatever he does shall prosper.*
>
> **Psalm 1:3**

That's you.

It's time to:

- **Think like royalty**
- **Live like an heir**
- **Give like a steward**
- **Walk like a partner with Heaven**

You are not ordinary.

You are not random.

You are not late.

You are not lacking.

You are positioned. Now prosper.

Overflow is not just a goal—it's your **God-given realm**. It's sustained through posture, prepared through structure, and multiplied through stewardship.

You were born for this.

You're not stepping into a season—you're stepping into your **Kingdom nature.**

Now go—and live like it.

CHAPTER 15

FINAL WORDS OF WEALTH AND WISDOM

CHAPTER FIFTEEN

FINAL WORDS OF WEALTH AND WISDOM

From Information to Impartation—Now Walk It Out

You've come far. You've learned. You've been stretched. You've been activated. This book was never just about financial information—it was always about **prophetic impartation**.

You haven't just read a book—you've taken a **journey into divine wealth**.

- From poverty mindsets to Kingdom authority
- From hustling to covenant alignment

- From fear to supernatural expectation
- From begging to boldness
- From survival to **overflow**

Isaiah 55:11 says,

So is My word that goes out from My mouth: It will not return to Me empty...

Isaiah 55:11

The words in this book were spirit and life. They were designed to **awaken what God planted in you** long ago.

You're not the same person who started Chapter One. You are now standing as a **possessor of divine insight, spiritual wealth, and financial authority.**

Now it's your turn to respond.

Don't just highlight pages—**highlight your habits.** Don't just quote truths—**start walking in them.**

This book was never meant to sit on your shelf. It was meant to:

- **Activate your destiny**
- **Reset your financial expectations**

- **Break cycles of delay and lack**
- **Push you into new realms of stewardship, faith, and impact**

James 1:22 exhorts,

> *Be doers of the word, and not hearers only...*

James 1:22

Let this be your **line in the sand.**

From this point forward, may you **live intentionally, give strategically, receive boldly, and prosper continually.**

Warfare, Wisdom, and Wealth with a Pure Heart

Make no mistake—**resistance will come.**

The enemy doesn't mind you being religious, as long as you remain:

- Bound financially
- Fearful of increase
- Distracted by survival

226

- Disconnected from your Kingdom assignment

But when you rise into divine wealth with clarity and covenant, **you become dangerous**.

Expect opposition. But never fear it.

- You are **equipped with revelation**
- You are **anointed for breakthrough**
- You are **backed by covenant**
- You are **rooted in truth**
- You are **surrounded by angelic help**

Isaiah 54:17 declares,

> *No weapon formed against you shall prosper...*
>
> **Isaiah 54:17**

Don't slow down when resistance comes. **Speed up. Push forward. Keep sowing. Keep building. Keep declaring.**

You're not just trying to be wealthy. **You're enforcing a Kingdom agenda.**

Guard your heart as you rise.

The danger of wealth is not in having it—it's in forgetting who gave it.

- Stay **humble**: always remember where He brought you from
- Stay **holy**: don't trade your soul for your goals
- Stay **hungry**: never stop learning, growing, and giving
- Stay **heaven-focused**: don't let possessions possess you

1 Timothy 6:17 reminds us,

Command those who are rich... not to be arrogant nor to put their hope in wealth...

1 Timothy 6:17

Purity preserves prosperity.

As God lifts you:

- Let worship rise higher than your bank balance
- Let surrender go deeper than your influence
- Let character run ahead of your increase

You are not just called to be rich—you are called to be **righteous and relevant in the Kingdom.**

Commissioned to Prosper with Purpose

This is your **Kingdom identity**:

You are not just a Christian with money—you are a **Kingdom financier**.

You are:

- A **distributor of divine resources**
- A **breaker of generational poverty**
- A **builder of spiritual and economic legacies**
- A **funder of visions, churches, missions, and movements**
- A **voice of wisdom in the marketplace**

You are called to **carry wealth with holiness, handle resources with revelation, and multiply abundance with purpose**.

This is not just about you—it's about the **generations after you,** the souls connected to your giving, and the Kingdom systems waiting on your obedience.

You are anointed for this. You are built for this. **You are chosen for this.**

Now is the time to move from information to activation.

- **Go**—step into your season boldly

- **Rise**—shake off limitation and small thinking
- **Build**—structures, businesses, ministries, and platforms
- **Fund**—churches, outreaches, schools, and Kingdom ideas
- **Prosper**—without guilt, fear, or apology

Romans 8:19 says,

The earnest expectation of the creation eagerly waits for the revealing of the sons of God.

Romans 8:19

And part of that revealing is the rise of **sons who walk in divine wealth**.

You are not behind. You are not unworthy. You are not disqualified. You are **positioned, equipped,** and **commissioned**.

Let the journey begin.

Welcome to a new dimension. You are no longer just praying for wealth—you are **partnering with God to steward it.**

Final Words of Wealth and Wisdom

You are not just chasing success—you are **manifesting Kingdom economy.**

And from this moment forward... **you will never be the same again.**

Final Declaration:

I am not ordinary.

I am a covenant child of God.

I walk in divine insight, divine supply, and divine strategy.

I do not chase money—money flows to me in alignment with purpose.

I do not beg for increase—I enforce it by obedience.

I do not hoard wealth—I multiply it, steward it, and release it for the Kingdom.

I am not afraid to prosper. I am not ashamed to rise.

I am empowered, equipped, and anointed for such a time as this.

I will fund revival. I will break cycles. I will build legacy.

I am a Kingdom financier.

And I will never be the same again.

CONCLUSION

We have come to the end of a book, but the beginning of a movement.

Decoding Divine Wealth was never intended to be just a teaching manual on finances. It is a divine manual for **transformation, elevation, and Kingdom mobilization.** Every chapter you've walked through has peeled back layers of spiritual truth, exposing what Heaven has always intended for you—not just financial increase, but complete alignment with your God-given purpose.

This book was a **summons to rise.** A prophetic call to stop settling for survival when you've been designed for stewardship, significance, and supernatural supply.

What You've Discovered:

- **Wealth begins with identity.** You are not a beggar—you are a son. A covenant heir. A steward of divine resources.

- **Prosperity is not greed—it's grace.** When rooted in purity and purpose, wealth becomes a tool to heal, build, and advance the Kingdom.

- **Abundance is not an accident—it's a result of alignment.** God funds what He authors. Provision flows when vision is clear and obedience is consistent.

- **Overflow is not a miracle—it is your covenant norm.** As long as you honor God's structure, cycles, and systems, increase will not just come—it will continue.

- **Inner healing matters.** A whole heart attracts holy wealth. God is more interested in your soul prospering than your bank account growing. But when the soul is healed, the hands are blessed.

Where You're Going:

From here, you're no longer just wishing for wealth—you're walking in **wisdom, strategy, and supernatural expectation.**

You are now equipped to:

- Create Kingdom-aligned wealth systems
- Multiply streams without losing spiritual focus
- Give generously, live righteously, and think generationally
- Fund visions, empower others, and break limitations
- Represent God well in the marketplace, ministry, and culture

You are now an answer to someone's prayer.

You are a **Kingdom financier**—called not just to make money, but to **move movements, mobilize missions**, and **multiply impact** in every sphere of influence.

What Must Never Be Forgotten:

- You are not blessed to impress—you are blessed to impact.

- You are not wealthy to boast—you are wealthy to build.
- You are not rich to compete—you are rich to complete God's work on the earth.
- You are not favored to isolate—you are favored to empower and uplift others.

This book has decoded Heaven's language concerning wealth. Now, your responsibility is to **walk in it, war with it**, and **worship through it**.

Let your life be the proof that it's possible to:

- Be wealthy and holy
- Be generous and grounded
- Be powerful and pure
- Be influential and humble
- Be Spirit-filled and financially free

Final Charge:

The world is waiting for people like you—those who carry vision in their hearts, revelation in their minds, and wealth in their hands.

Final Words of Wealth and Wisdom

The days of financial fear, limitation, and survival are over.

Now is the time to:

- Think differently
- Live boldly
- Sow strategically
- Build relentlessly
- And prosper unapologetically

You are not an accident.

You are an agent of divine economy.

And you will prosper—not by chance, but by covenant.

Now go—**and let the evidence of divine wealth be seen in your life.**

Welcome to your era of divine dominion.

DID YOU ENJOY THIS BOOK?

Did you enjoy reading this book? Do you know someone who can benefit from it? Feel free to share it with them with the following link:

https://lasouchpublishing.com/BishopRichard1

I would also appreciate it if you take a moment and leave an honest review for this book on Amazon. This helps others find the book and decide if this is a fit for them.

OTHER BOOKS BY THE AUTHOR

1. **Before You Say "I Do":** Spiritual Wisdom and Practical Counsel for Building a Marriage That Lasts
2. **The Secret Place:** Discovering the Hidden Realm of Intimacy, Power, and Divine Encounter
3. **Entrepreneurship:** Faith, Purpose & Prosperity - A Kingdom Guide to Building Profitable Businesses with Eternal Impact.
4. **Arsenals for Daily Living:** A Powerful Collection of Prayer Weapons for Everyday Victory
5. **Unshakable Confidence:** Breaking Fear, Embracing Identity, and Stepping Boldly into Destiny

Bishop
Richard Asamoah Boateng

Global Leader | Visionary Bishop |
Entrepreneur | Inspirational Speaker

ABOUT THE AUTHOR

Bishop Richard Asamoah Boateng

Global Leader | Visionary Bishop | Entrepreneur | Inspirational Speaker

Dr. Confidence, formally known as Bishop Richard Asamoah Boateng, is the Presiding Bishop of Destiny Impact Worship Centre and a distinguished leader with over 30 years of experience in ministry, business, and global influence. As a dynamic spiritual guide, entrepreneur, and strategic thinker, he has successfully directed private enterprises while serving as the President of multiple churches across international borders.

A highly sought-after speaker and leadership mentor, Dr. Confidence has a unique ability to connect, inspire, and transform lives through faith-based empowerment. His exceptional leadership and interpersonal acumen have allowed him to cultivate meaningful relationships with diverse stakeholders, including government officials, business executives, and community leaders.

Renowned for his expertise in international relations and negotiations, he has played a pivotal role in bridging cultural and communication gaps, fostering unity, and championing initiatives that promote spiritual growth and social impact.

With a mission to empower individuals with unshakable confidence, Dr. Confidence continues to be a beacon of hope, wisdom, and transformational leadership—driving change, elevating minds, and shaping the next generation of global leaders.

You can connect with Bishop Richard Asamoah Boateng on social media through any of the following channels.